A TISSUE OF LIES

Eudora Welty and the Southern Romance

Jennifer Lynn Randisi

UNIVERSITY
PRESS OF
AMERICA

LANHAM • NEW YORK • LONDON

Copyright © 1982 by

University Press of America,™ Inc.

4720 Boston Way
Lanham, MD 20706

3 Henrietta Street
London WC2E 8LU England

Library of Congress Cataloging in Publication Data

Randisi, Jennifer Lynn.

    Bibliography: p.
    Includes index.
    1. Welty, Eudora, 1909–   –Criticism and
interpretation. 2. Southern States in literature. 3. American
literature–Southern States–History and criticism. I.
Title.
PS3545.E6Z85   813'.52   82–45042
ISBN 0–8191–2451–6   AACR2
ISBN 0–8191–2452–4 (pbk.)

All University Press of America books are produced on acid-free
paper which exceeds the minimum standards set by the National
Historical Publications and Records Commission.

to Theodore and Josephine Randisi

CONTENTS

v

INTRODUCTION

Any examination of the relationship between the novels[1] of Eudora Welty and the Southern Romance tradition[2] must be an outgrowth, to a certain extent, of those definitions of the American Romance supplied by such critical works as Richard Chase's The American Novel and Its Tradition and Daniel G. Hoffman's Form and Fable in American Fiction,[3] as well as the primary documents of the nineteenth century. In his Custom House preface to The Scarlet Letter, for example, Hawthorne suggests that romance depends in part on treatment of subject rather than choice of subject.

> ... A child's shoe; the doll, seated in her little wicker carriage; the hobby-horse; -- whatever, in a word, has been used or played with during the day, is now invested with a quality of strangeness and remoteness, though still almost as vividly present as by daylight. Thus, therefore, the floor of our familiar room has become a neutral territory, somewhere between the real world and fairy-land, where the Actual and the Imaginary may meet, and each imbue itself with the nature of the other.[4]

Romance, according to Hawthorne, depends upon the interpretation of history (the Actual) and fiction (the Imaginary). Hawthorne's Actual is, at a basic level, any given location or backdrop. It is what Welty means by "place" -- a geographic grid on which photographs taken over time are superimposed. While the Actual redefines parameters, the Imaginary illuminates what happens within them. Therefore, the Imaginary is not event per se, but the interpretation or version of event as translated by the writer or story-teller. Together, location (a form of the Actual) and interpretation of event (a form of the Imaginary) create a "neutral territory" accountable neither solely in terms of the place to be illuminated nor the illumination itself. To use Northrop Frye's formulation, romance is a verbal imitation that exists midway between events (in time) and ideas (in mental space).[5] It is only in the conjunction of the two that the romance is created, in much the same way that the conjunction of moon and sun create an eclipse. What is viewed in each is a doubling in which the combination of two elements creates a dissimilar third. It is what Welty means when she refers to <u>The Robber Bridegroom</u> as a historical novel, but "not a historical historical novel."[6] It is a romance that partakes of event as well as what Welty would call "embroidery," and is, in effect, a transformation of history into story.

Perhaps the earliest and certainly the best examples of this blend of location and interpretation of event in American letters are in the Southern diarists Frances Anne Kemble, Judith W. McGuire, Ada Sterling, Eliza Francis Andrews, Mrs. Burton Harrison, Kate Stone, Sarah Morgan Dawson, and Mary Boykin Chesnut. Writing from the 1830s to the 1870s, these women and their contemporaries recreated a legend of the South and its central historical event, the Civil War, that drew equally on the Actual and the Imaginary. Of these war-time Southern chroniclers Ellen Glasgow has written:

> The war has been their apology and
> their defense, and they have trea-
> sured their version of the war
> record as the final and authentic
> flash of a legend to which time has
> not always been kind.[7]

The diary form itself suggests both an attempt at reportage and at a cataloging of interpretive response. As Sarah Morgan Dawson puts it in an August 3rd entry of her diary, "if I kept a diary of events, it would be one tissue of lies."[8] The diary is a form suggesting doubleness in that its attempts are ambiguous if not contradictory, and allow for a great deal of stylistic and thematic variation. Judith McGuire's <u>Diary of a Southern Refugee During the War</u>, for example, is the anecdotal and conversational work of a woman sympathetic to the Southern cause and supportive of the system of slavery, while Mary Boykin Chesnut's <u>A Diary from Dixie</u> reveals an emotionally-charged sensibility in deep conflict about the fact of slavery and her relationship to it. Clearly, events recorded in these diaries in roughly the same location and time period cannot help but be illuminated by the writer in fundamentally different ways. Each diary is therefore a romance in Hawthorne's sense, "somewhere between the real world and fairy-land," where soldiers have the potential to double as cavaliers[9] and Southern ladies to exist both as capable women and as damsels in distress.[10] Stylistic variation among diaries indicates patriotism as well as skepticism, and attests to the difficulty of maintaining historicity in the face of moral outrage. The ultimate paradox of the Southern post-war stance from which many diarists wrote can be observed in the dedication with which William Gilmore Simms chose to preface his War Poetry of the South.

To the Women of the South

They have lost a cause, but they have made a triumph! They have shown themselves worthy of any manhood; and will leave a record which shall survive all the caprices of time. They have proved themselves worthy of the best womanhood, and, in their posterity, will leave no trace which shall be unworthy of the cause which is lost, or of the mothers, sisters and wives, who have taught such noble lessons of virtuous effort and womanly endurance.[11]

Robert A. Lively defines the paradox as one that confuses "the simple techniques of making repeated assurances that the South believed it was fighting for justice" with logic.[12] The need behind such assurances, a need in part answered by the Southern diarist, was to translate loss into victory.

The Civil War diarists are connected to the novels of Eudora Welty through the Southern Romance tradition, a medium of connection which influenced the diarists directly and helped to shape their version of events. Most critics who deal with the evolution of Southern fiction tend to agree that a significant romantic or cavalier bias emerged in Southern letters in the 1830s.[13] Although the plantation novel preceeded the dime novel by three decades,[14] both forms shared an emphasis on the historical presentation of "romances of love and warfare."[15] As early as 1835, when John Pendleton Kennedy's Horse Shoe Robinson, a Tale of the Tory Ascendency was published, the historical time-lag point of view introduced by Sir Walter Scott's Waverly

had been adopted by the South. Like Scott, who set
Waverly "60 yrs. since," Kennedy allowed fifty years
to elapse before the events of Horse Shoe Robinson,
"that being deemed," according to Kennedy, "the fair
poetical limit which converts tradition into truth."[16]
The popular success of ante-bellum fiction is aptly
demonstrated by the immediate familiarity of Howard
Mumford Jones's parody a century later.

> A thousand stories have created
> the legend that is the South. Way
> down upon the Suwanne River the
> sun shines bright on my old
> Kentucky home where, bound for
> Louisiana, Little Eva has a banjo
> on her knee, and Old Black Joe,
> Uncle Remus and Miss Sally's
> little boy listen to the mocking-
> bird and watch a sweet chariot
> swing low one frosty morning! The
> gallant Pelham and his comrades
> bend forever over the hands of
> adorable girls in crinoline; under
> the duelling oaks Colonel Carter
> of Cartersville and Marse Chan
> blaze away at each other with
> pistols by the light of the
> silvery moon on Mobile Bay. It
> matters little now, Lorena, the
> past is in the eternal past, for I
> saw thee once, once only, it was on
> a July midnight and the full-orbed
> moon looked down where a despot's
> heel is on thy shore, Maryland, my
> Maryland.[17]

What we hear behind the passage, and therefore what
makes the passage work, is the Southern Romance
tradition.

Because Welty is not, like the ante-bellum
writers, an unself-conscious transmitter of the
Southern Romance, her novels are based on a manipulation of major thematic and stylistic elements inherent
to the tradition.[18] Her ironic effectiveness in the
habit of Bonnie Dee's magazine reading, for example,
just as William Faulkner's evocative description of the
Sartoris library in The Unvanquished,[19] depends upon
the manipulation of a traditional element -- in this
case, the tastes and educational superiority of the

x

ante-bellum Southerner. The constituent elements of the Southern Romance are the following:

1. reference to mythology born of, as John Crowe Ransom puts it, "classical and humanistic learning"[20]
2. regional mythology surrounding the Southern character
3. geographic legend and folk-tale growing out of localities such as the Natchez Trace
4. inter- and intra-family graphing or hierarchical structuring on the basis of myth as perpetuated by the Southern family
5. preoccupation with identity or name in relation to the first families of the South
6. acceptance of narrator or story-teller as authority
7. repetition of, and preoccupation with, incident (whether the Civil War or a bit of family history)
8. belief in the ability of language to order chaos and the need to rewrite Southern history

The first element, classical mythology, is a way of compounding the present with antiquity. For the Southern diarists, the use of Greek myth served to connect a crucial historical event in the present with a past tradtion. The identification provided a mythic context, a way of understanding an otherwise incomprehensible Civil War. The ante-bellum mind was predisposed to the classics well before the 1860s. A vogue for Greek revival architecture preoccupied the South from 1815 to the 1850s, and the ideal of "Athenian democracy" had long informed the Southerner's view of politics.[21] President Jefferson Davis was the archtypic Confederate and his home in Richmond, described by his wife Virginia Howell Davis in July, 1861, was in keeping with the Greek ideal.

The Carrara marble mantels were the delight of our children. One

was a special favorite of them, on
which the whole pilaster was
covered by two lovely figures of
Hebe and Diana, one on either side
in bold relief, which, with
commendatory taste, were not
caryatides ... The entablature
was Apollo in his chariot, in
basso relievo. Another was a
charming conception of Cupid and
Psyche, with Guido's Aurora for
the entablature.[22]

Classical identification carried to the battlefield as
well. General "Stonewall" Jackson, for example, was
eulogized in "Jackson, the Alexandria Martyr" for his
"more than Roman soul,"[23] and in "Coercion: A Poem for
Then and Now," John B. Thompson of Virginia fused the
battles of Greece with those of the South.

But, if smitten with blindness and
    mad with the rage
The gods gave to all whom they
    wished to destroy
You would act a new Iliad, to
    darken the age
With horrors beyond what is told
    us of Troy--[24]

If the South believed it was fighting the battles of
antiquity, then what it sought to preserve through
victory was the existence of an empire. In his novel
Among the Pines, James Roberts Gilmore had explained
the aims of "the Knights of the Golden Circle" as an
attempt to found "an empire that will be able to defy
all Europe -- one grander than the world has seen since
the age of Pericles."[25] This sort of classical
identification served to analogize, and therefore to
render comprehensible, the Civil War. It was a way of
problem-solving as James L. Adams defines the term, a
way of "bringing order to chaos."[26]

The constant identification with classical
mythology found in the Southern diaries is, in part, a
way of reaching through time and space to locate what
is repetitive and significant in human action. The
need to locate patterns is, as Kenneth E. Boulding,
President for the National Association for the Advance-
ment of the Sciences, has lately recognized, one that
seeks to "represent some kind of correspondence, a one-

to-one mapping as the mathematicians say, of some structure inside the human head with the structures of the universe."[27] In her use of the Cupid and Psyche myth as an envelope for the action of The Robber Bridegroom and her use of Yeats's poem "The Song of the Wandering Aengus" as a frame of reference for The Golden Apples, Welty is illustrating the same mode of identification to the core significance of human behavior. The effect of linkages of this sort is a doubling that forces the reader to view the situations presented in the narrative through a mythological transparency.[28]

Regional mythology functions in much the same way as classical, but with a narrower focus. Here, the myths are strictly those of the South as distinguished from the North and the rest of the world. They also transcend time, but not place because their subject is place as seen through time.[29] The process, defined by Alexander Karanikas in Tillers of a Myth: Southern Agrarians as Social and Literary Critics, is a "cultural relativism" not unlike that of T. S. Eliot "which justifies certain practices regardless of their being good or evil simply because they exist in an accepted social system."[30] In a sense, therefore, regional mythology is an inheritance and it is comprised, in the South, of the "trinity: nature, religion, myth."[31] John Crowe Ransom spoke for the Agrarians and perhaps for the South when he adapted T. S. Eliot's famous statement of principles: "I would court a program going something like this: In manners aristocratic, in religion, ritualistic; in art, traditional."[32]

Ransom's program is essentially not that far removed from the sentiment of Tyrtaeus when he wrote "The Voice of the South" nearly a century earlier.

> Oh, sound to awaken the dead from
>   their graves,
> The will that would thrust us from
>   place for our slaves,
> That, by fraud which lacks
>   courage, and plea that lacks
>   truth,
> Would rob us of right without
>   reason of truth.[33]

As late as the Civil War, in fact, Southerners were using the Sir Walter Scottian "Southron,"[34] and had effectively joined the cause of slavery with that of Southern womanhood.[35] Both were deeply rooted in the Southern soil. While ambivalent about her feelings during the conflict, Mary Boykin Chesnut could thus express the indomitable Southern pride typical of her generation of diarists ("Slavery has to go, of course, and joy go with it. These Yankees may kill us and lay waste to our land for a while, but conquer us -- never!"),[36] and Sarah Morgan Dawson could go as far as to propose that "if Lincoln could spend the grinding season on a plantation, he would recall his proclamation."[37] It is not surprising, therefore, that the one diarist to stand apart on the issue of slavery was Frances Anne Kemble.[38] Of the myth of harmonious plantation life she writes,

> I know that Southern men are apt to
> deny the fact that they do live
> under an habitual sense of danger;
> but a slave population, coerced
> into obedience, though unarmed and
> half-fed, is a threatening source
> of constant insecurity, and every
> Southern woman to whom I have
> spoken on the subject has admitted
> to me that they live in terror of
> their slaves.[39]

Her comments regarding Southern belles[40] and cavaliers[41] are even more to the point, and serve to accentuate her uneasy presence in a land whose regional myths were fundamentally at odds with her own.

Regional, like classical myths, are important in their ability to compound the narrative by extending it over time. Unlike classical myths, however, they point toward what Robert B. Heilman would call the "Southern Temper"[42] or W. J. Cash would identify as "the mind of the South."[43] It is a character frozen in place and, as such, is, to borrow a phrase from Faulkner, a "living fairy tale"[44] of the actions of that character as viewed over time. As Welty puts it in her essay "Some Notes on River Country,"

> Whatever is significant and
> whatever is tragic in a place live
> as long as the place does, though
> they are unseen, and the new life
> will be built upon those things --
> regardless of commerce and the way

of rivers and roads and other vagrancies.[45]

Geographic legend and folktale exist in the same way as do regional mythologies -- through an oral tradition. The repetition of story, incident, and anecdote common to classical, regional, and local myth is what keeps the living fairy tale alive. I group Civil War personalities with figures of Mississippi legend under the banner "geographic legend and folktale" because it seems to me that the process both undergo in becoming part of the living fairy tale is essentially the same. Through repetition, both sets of legends are re-created and perpetuated as pieces in a much larger geographic legend belonging as strongly to the Civil War years as to the twentieth century. Thus, the atrocities of General "Beast" Butler were already as much a part of local legend to Sarah Morgan Dawson, writing in 1862,[42] as were those of the Harpe brothers to Eudora Welty writing nearly a century later. We are dealing with the interpenetration of history and fiction, whether the history be that of the Civil War or the Natchez Trace, whether the story-teller be recounting an event that happened two days or two decades in the past. Both events contribute to place (in this case, the hamlets and towns of the South) and, as Welty knows, will "live as long as the place does."

The presence of Civil War monuments in town squares and sculpted cemeteries throughout the South attest to the continuing belief, voiced by Mary Boykin Chesnut in 1861, that "at the bottom of our hearts we believe every Confederate soldier to be a hero, sans peur et sans reproche."[47] In their narratives, the Civil War diarists engaged in a myth-making process that converted the Confederate soldier to the man of "bluest blood; gentleman to the tips of his fingers; chivalry incarnate."[48] Watching a troop of Confederate prisoners in 1865 prompted Mary Boykin Chesnut to write the following:

> There they go, the gay and gallant
> few, doomed; the last gathering of
> the flower of Southern pride, to
> be killed, or worse, to a
> prison.[49]

These "martyrs to a holy cause,"[50] as another diarist termed them, were the generalized product of Civil War heroes such as General "Stonewall" Jackson, Joseph E. Johnston, Robert E. Lee, and J. E. B.

Stuart, whose unparalleled bravery, fine military genius, and faultless breeding became the legendary standard to which all other Confederate soldiers were elevated.[51]

Weaving through the legend of the Confederate soldier are those of the Mississippi River, with its flatboat heroes and bandits, and those of the Southern orator and politician. Because both combine rhetoric, excessive pride, and a fierce defense of "place," the two legendary types can be said to arise from the same Southern impulse toward ethnocentricity.[52] The flatboat braggadocio recorded by Mark Twain is thus surprisingly similar in intention and effect to the ante-bellum political "cult of Calhoun."[53] It is by the mythmaking process that John C. Calhoun, like Mike Fink and the Harpe brothers before him was, by his death in 1850, incorporated into the legendary landscape of the South.

The smallest, but perhaps most significant, mythmaking unit is the family. Throughout the Civil War diaries and in Robert Manson Myers' monumental collection The Children of Pride: A True Story of Virginia and the Civil War[54] one senses the composite quality of an individual's life within the family. Mary Boykin Chesnut's portrait of the family patriarch, Colonel James Chesnut, Sr., for example, encompasses both the blind and deaf ninety-three year old man she sees in 1865 and "the Young Prince" he was known as in his youth.[55] Because the life of any member within the family is a process of accumulation, it is as rooted in time and place as are the other mythologies we have been discussing. And because family history is recalled and repeated by its members and members of other families, it becomes as significant a part of the living fairy tale as do the histories of General "Beast" Butler and the Harpe brothers. Family myths are those repeated most often because they are literally the closest to home. As Welty puts it in speaking of her own life, "except for what's personal, there is really so little to tell."[56] It is in the telling of what is personal that history is translated into story.[57]

Family myth and individual identity are closely related.[58] Family heroes like Jack Renfro of Losing Battles and George Fairchild of Delta Wedding are viewed within the family in much the same way as Colonel James Chesnut, Sr., is viewed by his grandson's wife, and the viewpoint cannot help but to affect the

way in which the "hero" comes to regard himself. In
Losing Battles, for example, although the myth
surrounding Jack Renfro bears no relation to the actual
events of his life, it nevertheless forms the substance
of his identity. During the reunion in which the novel
is set, Jack's family defends him both over his younger
brother Vaughn (himself much closer to the hero than
Jack) and against various conflicting perceptions that
surface throughout the day. Jack, in effect, becomes a
composite not only of his past and present, but also of
the versions of that past and present held by the
members of his immediate family and attending
relatives.

The link between name and identity extends beyond
the individual. In the Civil War diaries, for example,
name and location often stand for a complete index of
geographic, socio-political, economic, and even
ethical factors. Mrs. Burton Harrison's Recollections
Grave and Gay[59] begins as follows:

> My father was Archibald Cary,
> of Carysbrooke -- all old-time
> Virginians loved to write them-
> selves down as part of their
> parental estates -- son of Wilson
> Jefferson Cary, a nephew of Thomas
> Jefferson, whose marriage with
> Miss Virginia Randolph had taken
> place at Monticello.

Mrs. Harrison has, in the first sentence of her
narrative, rooted her family in place, social standing,
and political ideology. This kind of blanket identification with a "house" (in this case, the Jefferson line
of Monticello) is pervasive throughout the diaries, and
forms a mythos of generalization based on biography.
The identification is a shorthand for locating an
individual or family on a community map of local and
perhaps regional values. It is through such identification that General George H. Thomas, a superb military
leader whose reputation remained spotless through and
after the Civil War, never held the trust of the Union
and its leaders because he was "a Virginian who had
elected to remain in the United States Army."[60]   In
Welty's The Ponder Heart, Edna Earle similarly relies
on immediate identification, but a form that fills out
her narrative through a process of name-dropping. The
following char-acterization, which occurs early in the
story, is not at all unusual: "Miss Teacake Magee is

of course a Sistrunk (the Sistrunks are all Baptists -- big Baptists) and Professor Magee's widow."[61] None of the three facts given in this passage touch on Miss Teacake Magee's essential being, yet all serve to place her within the town of Clay through identification not only with the Sistrunk, but also with the Magee family.

The plotting of identity through name has another function both in the Civil War diaries and in the novels of Eudora Welty, and that is to establish the authority of the narrative voice. One of the hopes implicit in Mrs. Harrison's identification with Jefferson is that the reader will assume a certain honesty and credibility from the relation, even if one by marriage. In order to subscribe to her version of the events of the Civil War, the reader must accept Mrs. Harrison as a historian of sorts. The irony is, of course, that in formulating familial alliances Mrs. Harrison becomes a subjective historian, in effect, a romancer. This irony is more apparent in The Ponder Heart and illustrates the paradox of relying on an essentially unreliable narrative voice. Although Edna Earle's narration is idiosyncratic and highly colored by the way in which she perceives events, the reader has no choice but to accept her telling of the tale as well as the tale itself. Again, in dealing with both diary and novel, it is necessary to view the narrator as a participant observer, a historian as well as an interpreter of event.

Anecdotal identification is as capable of illuminating character as naming. Colonel James Chesnut's manner of bowing to a lady, and an officer's knack of casually tossing flowers into the laps of pretty Southern belles are gestures that typify the characters of these men to their writers. The actions gain significance in repetition, so that they become a signature. Gesture is often recalled within the context of anecdote. In The Ponder Heart, for example, the Peacock family can be dispensed with as soon as one understands that they "were the kind of people keep the mirror outside the house, and wave at trains till the day they die."[62] Similarly, Charlie Roy Hugg of Losing Battles can be encapsulated in the following: "Drunk and two pistols. Makes his wife answer the phone."[63] Here, as in the process of naming, the technique is one of an incisive verbal shorthand that both summons and dismisses the personality at hand. Other instances of anecdote, however, may point toward the serious as well as the comic in human nature and often form the central episode around which the narrative circles. In The Robber Bridegroom, the discovery of identity enacted by Rosamond and recalled from the myth of Cupid and Psyche is the action repeated in varying forms throughout the novel; in Delta Wedding, the focus is George's rescue of Maureen as viewed by several members of the Fairchild family; in The Ponder Heart, the ultimate significance of Uncle Daniel Ponder is captured in the tableau Edna Earle creates of him, flinging money to a stunned courtroom. Whether mentioned once or recalled throughout the narrative, identification by gesture and action is as important in determining identity as name.

In treating the belief in language to order chaos it will be necessary to return to the notion that the romancer transforms history into story. Although the diarists are more self-conscious narrators, Welty's narratives each have their own voice or mesh of voices. In The Robber Bridegroom, for example, one hears the language of the märchen as it weaves other voices into the final pattern of the novel. This primary voice is the transforming one that synthesizes the classical and regional mythology, legend and folktale, into a unified whole. Like that of the diarists, the language of the märchen is what orders the narrative. The ordering voice of Losing Battles, on the other hand, is lyric, yet it, too, synthesizes contradictory voices. The primary voices of The Robber Bridegroom and Losing Battles, like those of Delta Wedding, The Golden Apples, and The Optimist's Daughter, are stylistic and mediating rather than confidentially personal, as are those of the participant observers encountered in the diaries and The Ponder Heart. The secondary voices of minor participant observers (such as Uncle Percy's version of Jack Renfro's history in Losing Battles) account for the compounded vision of history contained in each work. Because each voice is a different filter of experience, a separate point of view from which to regard event, each voice recreates and reshapes history into the living fairy tale. Versions are either reinforced or recast in repetition, thereby creating their own separate "truths." It is thus ultimately narrative voice and language itself that create the Southern Romance. For language, as Edward Sapir knows, is more than a system of thought transference. Combined, languages "are invisible garments that drape themselves about our spirit and give a predetermined form to all its symbolic expression. When the expression is of unusual significance, we call it literature."[64] It is with the element of language that we return to Hawthorne's notion that romance depends, in part, on the treatment of subject rather than the choice of subject.

Having defined the elements inherent to the Southern Romance, we must now locate them within the novels themselves. Chapters two through six study the novels chronologically, beginning with The Robber Bridegroom (1942) and ending with The Optimist's Daughter (1972). With minor exceptions, each chapter focuses on all of the elements listed above as they appear within the novel at hand.

NOTES

[1]Although Ruth M. Vande Kieft has convincingly argued that The Golden Apples is indeed a novel rather than a collection of short stories (Eudora Welty. New York: Twayne Publishers, Inc., 1962), the many excellent myth studies of the work render another treatment of its constituent elements unnecessary.

[2]The term is here distinguished from the tradition of "Southern literature," which has been recently defined by Benjamin Forkner and Patrick Samway, S.J. (Stories of the Modern South. New York: Bantam Books, 1977) as the outgrowth of "an environment where states' rights are important; where the Bible is read, memorized, and cherished; where decentralized government is seen as something valuable; where families tend to live by traditional agricultural means; where a code of honor and polite manners have been traditionally expected of everyone; where Elizabethan literature and the works of Sir Walter Scott were esteemed for decades; and where slavery and the effects of the Civil War have left a definite mark on mores and attitudes" (p.x).

[3]It will be recalled that Chase's focus here is on what he terms the "trans-Jamesian" realm of fiction in which romance arises from and modifies the realistic novel. Hoffman, like Chase, recognizes the American romancer's use of allegory, myth, and ritual over what he terms "presumptive realism."

[4]"The Custom House" introduction to The Scarlet Letter (New York: New American Library, 1959), p. 45.

[5]Northrop Frye, "New Directions from Old," Myth and Mythmaking. Ed. Henry A. Murray (New York: George Braziller, Inc., 1960), p. 119.

[6]Eudora Welty, "Fairy Tales of the Natchez Trace." The Eye of the Story (New York: Random House, 1978), p. 311.

[7]Robert A. Lively, Fiction Fights the Civil War: An Unfinished Chapter in the Literary History of the American People (Chapel Hill: The University of North Carolina Press, 1957), p. 36.

[8]_A Confederate Girl's Diary_ (Bloomington: Indiana University Press, 1960), p. 139.

[9]Identification with the cavalier extended beyond the Confederate soldier. Of those responsible for the Klan Constitution (1867), for example, Rollin G. Osterweis writes: "Its authors were violent, resolute, purposeful men on the one hand, and almost childishly romantic adolescents on the other -- a combination of qualities typical of the Southern cult of chivalry." _The Myth of the Lost Cause, 1867-1900_ (Hamden, Conn.: The Shoe String Press, 1973), p. 18. For a complete study of the cavalier see William R. Taylor's _Cavalier & Yankee: The Old South and the American National Character_ (New York: Harper & Row, 1957).

[10]For comprehensive treatment of this theme see Anne Firor Scott's _The Southern Lady: From Pedestal to Politics, 1830-1930_ (Chicago: The University of Chicago Press, 1970). That the ideal of womanly perfection was difficult, at best, to maintain, is evidenced by the Biblical verse Scott found quoted most often in private diaries: "The heart is deceitful above all things and desperately wicked: Who can know it?" (Jeremiah 17:9), p. 11.

[11]William Gilmore Simms, _War Poetry of the South_ (New York: Richardson & Co., 1866).

[12]_Fiction Fights the Civil War_, p. 53.

[13]Rollin G. Osterweis traces the growth of a nationalistic romanticism to January of 1831, when Garrison's _Liberator_ began publication, to Nat Turner's slave insurrection in Southampton County, Virginia, later the same year, and to increased participation by Southerners between 1831 and 1850 in the Cult of Chivalry (the hallmarks of which included the hunt, the role of the horse in tournaments, the race, and an emphasis on heraldry, ancestry, and romantic place-naming). _Romanticism and Nationalism in the Old South_ (New Haven: Yale University Press, 1949), pp. 54-55. William R. Taylor, on the other hand, looks to the initial rise of the plantation novel (from 1832 to the mid-1850s), and most particularly to the substance and success of John Pendleton Kennedy's _Swallow Barn_ (1832), for insight into the literary evolution of the Southern aristocrat: "John Pendleton Kennedy, more than anyone else, succeeded in trans-

porting the squire to America" (<u>Cavalier & Yankee</u>, p. 181).

[14]Edmund Pearson (<u>Dime Novels; Or, Following an Old Trail in Popular Literature</u>. Port Washington, New York: Kennikat Press, Inc., 1929) dates publication of the first dime novel as June of 1860 (p. 13).

[15]Ibid., p. 8.

[16]Robert A. Lively, <u>Fiction Fights the Civil War</u>, p. 19.

[17]Howard Mumford Jones, "On Leaving the South." <u>Scribner's</u>, LXXXIX (Jan. 1931), p. 25.

[18]One of the differences between the unself-conscious and the self-conscious author is the use of irony. A novel like <u>The Ponder Heart</u>, for example, depends upon the triangulation between listener, Edna Earle, and reader. For the modern novelist of the South irony lies, as Scholes and Kellogg have noted of the modern novelist in general (<u>The Nature of Narrative</u>. London: Oxford University Press, 1966), "not between author or narrator and character, but between limited understanding which is real and an ideal of absolute truth which is itself suspect" (p. 277).

[19]William Faulkner, <u>The Unvanquished</u> (New York: Vintage Books, 1934), p. 18.

[20]John Crowe Ransom, "Reconstructed but Unregenerate." <u>I'll Take My Stand: The South and the Agrarian Tradition</u> (New York: Harper, 1930), p. 14.

[21]Osterweis, <u>Romanticism and Nationalism in the Old South</u>, pp. 108-9.

[22]<u>Heroines of Dixie: Spring of High Hopes</u>. Ed. Katherine M. Jones (New York: Ballentine Books, 1955), p. 71.

[23]<u>War Poetry of the South</u>, p. 51.

[24]<u>War Poetry of the South</u>, p. 47-8.

[25]<u>Fiction Fights the Civil War</u>, p. 82.

[26]James L. Adams, Conceptual Blockbusting (San Francisco: San Francisco Book Co., 1976), p. 55.

[27]"The Sciences and the Humanities: Kindred Activities." Humanities Report, May 1979, Vol. 1, No. 5.

[28]It may be useful at this point to clarify "myth." Throughout this study, I will be using the definition supplied by Scholes and Kellogg in The Nature of Narrative, where mythos stands for "a traditional story" (p. 12). Myth is able to serve as an element of the Southern Romance by constituting the building blocks out of which it is constructed. The power of myth to alter event is overwhelming. As Ernst Cassirer writes (The Philosophy of Symbolic Forms, 3 Vols., New Haven: Yale University Press, 1955. Trans. Ralph Manheim. Vol. 2, Mythical Thought): it is "not by its history that the mythology of a nation is determined, but, conversely, its history is determined by its mythology" (p. 5).

[29]Regional mythology is connected to that of the family. It is this connection that informs Evelyn D. Ward's The Children of Bladensfield During the Civil War (New York: Viking Press, 1978), written for "the great-grandchildren and the great-great-grandchildren of the old place, and for all thoughtful people who know what a mighty help history, heart learned, is to the present," and that Andrew Lytle recognizes in "The Working Novelist and the Mythmaking Process" (Myth and Mythmaking): "family and place, as I have said, go together. It was the sense of both which set the South apart in this country" (p. 142).

[30]Ibid., p. 92.

[31]Ibid., p. 155.

[32]Ibid., p. 164.

[33]War Poetry of the South, p. 33

[34]Romanticism and Nationalism in the Old South, pp. 46-7. See also War Poetry of the South, pp. 17, 26, 60.

[35]As Henry Timrod put it in "A Cry to Arms": "We battle for our country's right, / And for the lily's sake!" War Poetry of the South, p. 51.

[36]Mary Boykin Chesnut, _A Diary from Dixie_. Ed. Isabella D. Martin, Myrta Lockett Avary. (New York: D. Appleton & Co., 1905), p. 74.

[37]_A Confederate Girl's Diary_, p. 277.

[38]Although written well before the Civil War, Kemble's _Journal of a Residence on a Georgia Plantation 1838-1839_ (Chicago: Afro-Am Press, 1969) was originally published in 1863 in an effort to influence British opinion regarding the war.

[39]_Journal of a Residence_, p. 295.

[40]"I pity them for the stupid sameness of their most vapid existence, which would deaden any amount of intelligence, obliterate any amount of instruction, and render torpid and stagnant any amount of natural energy and vivacity. I would rather die -- rather a thousand times -- than live the lives of these Georgia planters' wives and daughters." _Journal of a Residence_, p. 156.

[41]"If the accounts given by these ladies of the character of the planters in this part of the South may be believed they must be as idle, arrogant, ignorant, dissolute, and ferocious as that medieval chivalry to which they are fond of comparing themselves." _Journal of a Residence_, p. 286.

[42]Robert B. Heilman, "The Southern Temper." _Hopkins Review_, 6, (Fall 1952).

[43]W. J. Cash, _The Mind of the South_ (New York: Knopf, 1941).

[44]William Faulkner, _Absalom, Absalom!_ (New York: Modern Library, 1936), p. 76.

[45]Eudora Welty, "Some Notes on River Country." _The Eye of the Story_, p. 299.

[46]_A Confederate Girl's Diary_, p. 35.

[47]_A Diary from Dixie_, p. 95.

[48]Ibid., p. 43.

[49]Ibid., p. 371.

[50] A Southern Reader. Ed. William Thorp (New York: Knopf, 1955), p. 100.

[51] See Lt. Col. Joseph B. Mitchell, Military Leaders in the Civil War (New York: G. P. Putnam's Sons, 1972) for the legends of Generals "Stonewall" Jackson (pp. 37-8, 40), Joseph E. Johnston (p. 175), and Robert E. Lee (pp. 63, 86). For the legends surrounding General J. E. B. Stuart see Rollin G. Osterweis, The Myth of the Lost Cause, p. 12.

[52] See Life on the Mississippi (New York: The Heritage Press, 1944), particularly the speeches of the river raftsmen on pages 18-19.

[53] Romanticism and Nationalism in the Old South, p. 53.

[54] New Haven: Yale University Press, 1972.

[55] A Diary from Dixie, pp. 391-2.

[56] Ruth M. Vande Kieft, Eudora Welty, p. 15.

[57] The two types of family myth present in the Southern Romance (the intra- as well as inter-familial) are perhaps best demonstrated in the theme of brother against brother. In The Stories and Fables of Ambrose Bierce (Ed. Edward Wagenknecht. Owings Mills, Md.: Stemmer House, 1977), especially "A Horseman in the Sky" (pp. 29-37), War Poetry of the South (p. 59), and Fiction Fights the Civil War (p. 45), the impersonal drama of war is often subordinate to the intra- and inter-familial drama of divided loyalty.

[58] Robert Scholes and Robert Kellogg have stated that "the ritualistic romantic quest for the Grail is metamorphosed in modern fiction into the psychological search for identity" (The Nature of Narrative, p. 287). In the Southern Romance, the hero's search for identity is often complicated by definitions imposed by his family.

[59] New York: Scribner's, 1911.

[60] Mitchell, Military Leaders in the Civil War, p. 215.

[61] Eudora Welty, The Ponder Heart (New York: Harcourt, Brace & World, 1954), p. 14.

[62]Ibid., p. 20

[63]Eudora Welty, Losing Battles (New York: Random House, 1970), p. 50.

[64]Edward Sapir, Language: An Introduction to the Study of Speech (New York: Harcourt, Brace, Jovanovich, 1921), p. 221.

CHAPTER I. - THE ROBBER BRIDEGROOM

Perhaps no other Welty narrative combines elements of myth, legend, folktale, and regional mythology as successfully as The Robber Bridegroom. If we follow Daniel G. Hoffman's definition of the romancer as distinct from the novelist in her or his concern with myth, folktale, and ritual, then we can begin to see Welty's book not only as a romance, but more specifically as a Southern romance. John Peale Bishop, in his essay on The Robber Bridegroom, misinterprets this attempt to write within the tradition of the Southern romance as an attempt to establish the American tall tale as "our equivalent of the European folktale."[2] Welty's story, in fact, contains both tall tale[3] and folktale. It is precisely the conjunction of classical mythology, local legend, folktale motif, and Southern mythology that renders The Robber Bridegroom a triumph of the romantic tradition in the American grain.

The Robber Bridegroom functions as a Southern romance on both thematic and stylistic levels. The story's plot is an amalgamation, as many critics have noted, of the Cupid and Psyche myth and several of Grimm's tales including, among others, "The Robber Bridegroom," "Snow White and the Seven Dwarfs," and "Cinderella."[4] Several characters of local Mississippi legend, such as the Harpe brothers (shortened to Harp in Welty's tale) and Mike Fink, also weave in and out of the narrative, carrying the actual towns of Rodney, New Orleans, and Natchez from history into legend, and rendering the Natchez Trace the scene of mystery and danger that it appeared to be in the Southern oral tradition of the mid-1800s. With the central character, Clement Musgrove, local legend is compounded by the myth of the Southern planter and plantation owner, a benign innocent whose cotton crops flourish effortlessly.[5]

The language of the German märchen[6] is the stylistic device that places all of these elements within the thematic sphere of the fairy tale. Almost any paragraph from the text will serve to illustrate the sense of timeless and placeless enchantment[7] that the language of the märchen creates.

> ... Rosamond found herself before she knew it at the edge of the forest, and with the next step the

1

> house was out of sight. And she
> was still carrying the pail of
> milk in her hand.

Time disappears ("Rosamond found herself before she knew it at the edge of the forest") as does place ("with the next step the house was out of sight"). Yet time and place are present, paradoxically, beyond the stylistic framework of the märchen. That is, Rosamond is in a fairy tale that has the specific backdrop of Mississippi legend and Southern myth: we, as readers, do not lose sight of the fact that the forest is in Mississippi and that Rosamond's "house" is a plantation. This doubled stylistic screen of time/no time and place/no place is the genius of the book. We can see this technique more clearly in the juxtaposition of the medieval written tradition and the Southern oral tradition that is given early in the tale.

> ... Red as blood the horse rode the
> ridge, his mane and tail straight
> out in the wind, and it was the
> fastest kidnapping that had ever
> been in that part of the country.
> (pp. 64-65)

This sentence, split in half, illustrates both a medieval concern with alliteration and cadence, reading almost as two lines of poetry -- "red as blood the horse rode the ridge / his main and tail straight out in the wind" -- and a fragment of Southern folk legend -- "it was the fastest kidnapping that had ever been in that part of the country." The first half of the sentence is formal and stylized, the second, folksy and confidential, as if Welty were whispering a secret of Mississippi legend in the reader's ear.

The use of this doubled perspective is similarly evident in Welty's self-consciousness as artist. Near the end of the tale, Welty's voice can be heard behind that of Mike Fink, a tale-teller in his own right, admonishing Rosamond not to interfere in the creation of art: "'Hold back, Madame,' said the mail rider, 'for this is what happened to me and not to you, and it is my business whether the persimmons were ripe or not'" (p. 171). So, too, is it Welty's business whether or not the persimmons are ripe. In other words, the artist consciously rewrites myth, legend, folktale, and regional mythology into a new work of art, a new romance or tale. And it is this adaptation

2

of conventional and legendary elements that is important in treating The Robber Bridegroom within the doubled traditions of romance literature and Southern literature. If, as Mike Fink asserts, "this is what happened to me and not to you," then the "I" is the filter through which "what happened" is sifted and refined, whether myth, fairy tale, or legend. And in the sifting and refinement "what happened" becomes a story.

The primary adaptation, and one that serves as an envelope for the action of The Robber Bridegroom, is the myth of Cupid and Psyche. In the myth,[9] Psyche, a beauty and a virgin, is caught between the jealousy of Venus (whom she had usurped in beauty) and the help of various gods, including Zephyrus, who initially rescues her from Venus's wrath and sets her down in a valley complete with a well-stocked cottage and a nighttime lover-husband. Psyche is eventually persuaded by her jealous sisters to discover the identity of her husband, whose face she has never seen. Fearful that her child will be the offspring of a monster, she attempts the discovery one night by shining a lamp on her lover, thereby recognizing by light the face of Cupid. A drop from the lamp touches and wakes him, causing him to flee from her through the window. The lovers, after much wandering and substantial help from the gods, are eventually reunited, and live happily ever after.[10] In his study of folklore motifs, Stith Thompson has recorded several variations on the theme of an animal or supernatural husband. But the essential plot of a girl, married to a monster-husband, whose happiness is interrupted by a transgression on her part, appears in no other tale.

That Welty drew heavily on the components of this myth is evident in both her treatment of character and her use of narrative detail. Psyche's beauty, virginity, and curiosity are obviously mirrored in Rosamond, just as Cupid's beauty, secret identity, and the split between his daytime and nighttime worlds are reflected in the character of Jamie Lockhart. Welty gives us a précis of the myth midway through her tale.

> So Rosamond stayed and kept
> house for the robbers. And at
> first the life was like fairyland.
> Jamie was only with her in the
> hours of night, and rode away
> before the dawn, but he spoke as

> kind and sweet words as anyone
> ever could between the hours of
> sunset and sunrise. (p. 82)

Within this most basic correspondence, several details
scattered throughout the narrative function in
conjuring the myth of Cupid and Psyche without
retelling it. That is, the details appear within an
altered context so that the myth is evoked as merely
one screen through which the reader can view Welty's
tale. The wilderness cottage of the Cupid and Psyche
myth can therefore double as a wilderness robber den,
the three jealous sisters appear in the form of a
wicked stepmother, and the husband is transformed into
a robber-gentleman. Another detail, the window, is
important not only to Jamie, who, like Cupid, uses it
as a means of escape (p. 135), but also to Mike Fink
early in the tale (p. 18) and later to Rosamond, who
first anticipates Jamie's departure (p. 85) and then
tries to follow his escape (p. 135).

By far the most important motif borrowed from the
myth, however, is the association between the secluded
cottage and an Edenic -- that is, timeless and placeless -- paradise.[11]

> ... One day Jamie did not ride
> away with the others, and then the
> day was night and the woods were
> the roof over their heads. The
> tender flames of the myrtle trees
> and the green smoke of the cedars
> were the fires of their hearth. In
> the radiant noon they found the
> shade, and ate the grapes from the
> muscadine vines. The spice-dreams
> rising from the fallen brown pine
> needles floated through their
> heads when they stretched their
> limbs and slept in the woods. The
> stream lay still in the golden
> ravine, the water glowing darkly,
> the colors of fruits and nuts. (p.
> 86)

The lovers exist in perfect relation to nature: the
wilderness provides their food and shelter bountifully
and effortlessly. That Jamie recognizes the disparity
between the timeless paradise represented symbolically
in night[12] and the day-world of thievery and intrigue

4

is evident in his reasoning on the day he spends at home with Rosamond.

> For he thought he had it all divisioned off into time and place, and that many things were for later and for further away, and that now the world had just begun. (p. 87)

Jamie's identity as a bridegroom is timeless and placeless; it is archetypal in nature: his identity as a robber, on the other hand, is linked to a very specific time and place. The former is a mythic structure; the latter partakes of legend.

Like the Cupid and Psyche myth, Welty uses the circle to evoke a mythological context. According to Mircea Eliade, in his _Cosmos and History: The Myth of the Eternal Return_, the circle is a complex metaphor for eternal return. Thus, "everything begins over again at its commencement every instant. The past is but a prefiguration of the future. No event is irreversible and no transformation is final."[13] The circle is essentially a symbol of meaningful repetition. As Eliade puts it, "it alone confers a reality upon events."[14] The complex web of circular motions, encircling patterns, and circles themselves that Welty traces in _The Robber Bridegroom_ can be seen on one level, as the symbolic equivalent of her use of myth and folktale. Each circle, like each mythic and folkloristic motif, is a repetition of a general mythic truth or folkloristic reality that, when combined with the others, forms a kind of thematic concentricity. Thus, the story of Cupid/Jamie and Psyche/Rosamond is a circle set within the larger circle of Welty's adaptation. This relationship is accentuated in Rosamond's kipnapping when, swung by Jamie onto the back of the galloping Orion, the two are isolated from the rest of the world: "Up the ridge they went, and a stream of mist made a circle around them" (p. 63). The image is here a symbol of the relationship between Jamie and Rosamond -- isolate, inviolable, enchanted. The circle is completed, by the end of the tale, in marriage and the revelation of identity.

Circles also function as literal images traced by various of Welty's characters. The ever-present Indians, for example, threaten by encircling different characters throughout the narrative, and meet, as do

5

the robbers, in a circular pattern for judgment and decision-making (pp. 159, 130). In a sense, these circles are progressive in that they function in furthering the plot. The circles that are traced in confusion, however, are neither representative of progress nor of eternal return. These are "bewitching" circles, meaningless repetition. Rosamond, frazzled and overworked, appears "a poor bewitched creature that could only go in circles" (p. 68), and Clement, losing his way when pursuing Rosamond, feels himself "charging in a circle" (p. 105). Goat similarly whirls in a circle before Salome's displeasure (p. 59), the Indians' dogs run always in circles (p. 148), and Salome, intently thinking, paces a circle on the floor (p. 116). These circles counterpoint the theme of meaningful return by representing confusion, frustration, and even madness. They are the antithesis of progressive movement and therefore exist out of time in a vacuum or chaos.

The center of the circle is a symbol as important as the circle itself. According to Eliade, the center of the circle is the point at which heaven, earth, and hell meet.[15] As such, it is "the zone of absolute reality." Clement, the narrative center of the tale, places himself within a circle of stones before making his philosophical speech in chapter five (p. 141) and the Chief's son proclaims Salome's just fate from the center of a circle (p. 162). The murder of the Indian maiden, which leads to the Indians' revenge, occurs within the center of the robber circle (p. 130) and serves as the episode paralleled by Salome's death in the fifth chapter. In each episode a woman is judged by the center of a circle. Both women are murdered for revenge, and their deaths are witnessed by the members of that band.

By far the most important center, however, is Jamie himself. He is the locus toward which the other characters gravitate in chapter five.

> ... There he lay on the ground under a plum tree, napping away with a smile on his face, while the paths of the innocent Clement and the greedy Salome and the mad Little Harp and the reproachful Rosamond all turned like the spokes of the wheel toward this dreaming hub. (p. 146)

Jamie's identity is the central reality upon which the
story rests. It is in his mixed identity that the
elements of myth, legend, folktale, and Southern
mythology merge. He contains elements not only of
Cupid and the folkloristic supernatural husband, but
also, as we shall see, of the legendary Joseph Thompson
Hare and the Southern gentleman. In general terms,
Jamie is the hero of "space" as defined by R. W. B.
Lewis in The American Adam.[16] His domain is the area
of potentiality, the unbounded wilderness, which he
crosses and recrosses throughout the tale. He is the
unfettered traveler as Robert M. Coates defines him in
The Outlaw Years: The History of the Land Pirates of
the Natchez Trace.

> ...he went into the wilderness as
> if into a temporary oblivion, from
> which no word or other warning of
> his passing might be expected to
> ensue until he appeared again, at
> his destination.[17]

It is here, with the Natchez Trace, that the legendary
aspects of The Robber Bridegroom begin.

In the mid-1800s, the Trace was a 550-mile trail
leading from Nashville to Natchez. Although the most
dangerous segment of the Trace was a 300-mile strip
ruled by Choctaws and Chickasaws, the entire Trace was
legendary for its banditry and violence. Welty makes
this association in her first description of the Trace.

> ... And at the foot of this
> ravine ran the Old Natchez Trace,
> that trail where travelers passed
> along and were set upon by the ban-
> dits and the Indians and torn
> apart by the wild animals. (pp.
> 43-44)

Both well-traveled and dangerous, the Trace provides
the mixture of verisimilitude and mystery that charac-
terizes the book's tone. The Trace weaves in and out
of the tale in much the same way as the myth of Cupid
and Psyche, supplying a contextual setting within which
Mississippi legend is conjured and held. Because the
trace leads both to the woods and to the city, it is an
area of possibility where characters both lose their
way and find themselves.

7

Jamie Lockhart belongs as much to the Natchez Trace as he does to the cottage in the woods or the city. In his legendary aspects, he most closely resembles Joseph Thompson Hare,[18] a gentleman robber of Mississippi legend. Like Hare, Jamie obtains a passport (p. 19) which enables him to elude the law by crossing into the Louisiana territory: again like Hare, Jamie uses berry juice to increase the ferocity of his appearance and obscure his identity. The most striking parallels between the two, however, are in their ability to separate business and love. Hare, like Jamie, is a dandy. He robs intermittently, accumulating enough wealth to live comfortably in New Orleans until, penniless, he again turns to banditry. Like Jamie, Hare perceives a distinction between his two identities and carefully avoids complicating them. Charles C. Clark reads Jamie's easy transitions between these two identities as a deliberately ironic statement by Welty's narrator. His shifting, says Clark, "should dispel any ideas that Jamie is a conventional hero of romance. Like many people, Jamie can close his mind to unpleasantness in the past as well as in the present."[19] The flaw in Clark's analysis is precisely in trying to read Jamie as a conventional hero of romance. That he contains elements of the traditional hero is doubtless, but it is the synthesis of these with legendary elements that render Jamie a specifically Southern hero. Further, questions of "unpleasantness" signify a failure to understand the violent tradition of the Natchez Trace within which Welty is working.

The Harpe brothers, like Joseph Thompson Hare, are legendary Mississippi folk heroes who belong to this violent tradition. In their largest legendary context, Welty's Big and Little Harp bear a strong resemblance to their Mississippi counterparts. Both pairs are ferocious bandits who live by their wits along the Trace, identifying themselves after a crime by shouting "we are the Harp(e)s!" as they disappear into the woods.[20] Although references to Little Harp as both mad (p. 147) and ugly (p. 92) roughly correspond to Mississippi legend, his murder by Jamie is a literary invention. As legend has it, Little Harpe was hanged in 1804 and buried near the Trace. Welty's concern with this legend, however, begins much before Little Harpe's demise and just after Big Harpe's death. In the legend, Big Harpe was murdered several years before his brother, and his head was nailed to a tree, where it remained to provide the spot with the permanent name

of "Harpe's Head."[21] Welty changes the tree to a pole
and moves it, complete with the head of Big Harp, to
Rodney, from where Little Harp rescues it prior to the
action of the tale. The more important change,
however, is in animating this head, in making it
capable of talking (or rather quarreling) with Little
Harp. It is through this device that Welty transforms
the head from a legendary to a folk motif.

In a sense, Big Harp's head functions as the
visual representation of the theme of identity. At
first kept hidden away by Little Harp, the head is
passed through the phases of anonymity, recognition and
new identity. The head literally goes full circle in
an Eliadean cycle of eternal return: from a pole in
Rodney Square to a pole in Rodney Square. By the end
of the tale, when the head is posted as "Jamie
Lockhart, the Bandit of the Woods" (p. 155), Jamie's
identity and that of Big Harp have become synonymous.
That Jamie must forfeit either his identity of robber
or that of bridegroom is implied with Little Harp's
recognition of his identity earlier in the tale.

> 'Aha, but I know who you are
> too,' said Little Harp, sticking
> out his tongue in a point, and his
> little eyes shining. 'Your name
> is Jamie Lockhart and you are the
> bandit in the woods, for you have
> your two faces together and I see
> you both.'
>   At that, Jamie staggered back
> indeed, for he allowed no one who
> had seen him as a gentleman to see
> him as a robber, and no one who
> knew him as a robber to see him
> without the dark-stained face,
> even his bride. (p. 112)

Thus, it is Jamie's identity as a robber that is neatly
assumed by Big Harp's head in its return to Rodney
Square.

In the figure of Mike Fink, Welty again utilizes a
character of Mississippi legend -- in this case, a combination of the riverboat pirate and the mail rider --
to emphasize the theme of identity. When we first
encounter him in Welty's tale, Fink is the image of the
riverboat hero popular into the 1880s.

> Then, sailing his cap in the
> air, he gave a whistle and a shake
> and declared that he was none
> other than Mike Fink, champion of
> all the flatboat bullies on the
> Mississippi River, and was ready
> for anything. (p. 8)

He drinks, swaggers, and boasts his way through
Rodney's Landing and the first chapter of the tale,
then drops out of the narrative until the last chapter,
where he reappears as a secretive mail rider. It is
Fink's encounter with Jamie in this first significant
chapter that leads to his disgrace and lowered stature
as a mail rider along the Trace. His position, like
that of the Harps, is connected with the question of
identity. As a flatboat hero, Fink is anxious to identify himself to all he meets; as a mail rider, he is
reluctant to whisper his name to Rosamond. Although
Welty restores Fink to his former greatness beyond the
framework of the tale, she shakes his reputation and
takes his identity from him within it. These changes
in the Mike Fink legend allow Welty's character to
become both a thematic and stylistic envelope for The
Robber Bridegroom: it is the reassertion of shaken
identity that closes the tale, just as the initial
assertion of identity opened it.

Two other details of folk legend warrant mention
here, but in order to examine them we must return to
Clement's arrival in Rodney's Landing. Clement's
arrival is the arrival of peacefulness and honesty.
His almost ritualistic search through three inns for an
honest landlord is, in effect, a confrontation with the
realities of ear-clipping, the method employed to
punish landlord bandits in the 1880s. The effect of
this confrontation is not only to evoke the stark backdrop of the American frontier, but also to accentuate
Clement's innocent presence as a part of that backdrop.
By juxtaposing Clement and the innkeepers in the first
chapter, Welty creates an ambivalent landscape, one
composed both of peacefulness and violence, innocence
and dishonesty. The first chapter thus functions as
the establishing shot in a film: the initial frame
informs the whole. The tone of the book, like that of
the film, is visible in this initial contact; the
reader, like the viewer, knows what kind of offering to
expect.

The sense of enchantment noted earlier in the
discussion of the language of the märchen is as signi-

10

ficant in this first chapter as are those of peaceful-
ness/innocence and violence/dishonesty. Because
Welty's descriptions form an integral part of this
sense, it is worth re-examining one of them in some
detail. The book is extremely visual both in the
quantity and quality of the almost surrealistic movement of objects, animals, and plant life. A passage
from page 2 will serve as an example.

As his foot touched shore,
the sun sank into the river the
color of blood, and at once a wind
sprang up and covered the sky with
black, yellow, and green clouds
the size of whales, which moved
across the face of the moon.

The sun sinks, almost magically, at the touch of
Clement's foot on shore; the wind springs up and
covers, as if it has become a wild beast; clouds are
linked with whales that swim across the moon. As in a
Chagall painting objects, such as the flying cow of
Mobile encountered in chapter 2, are taken out of
context and assigned unlikely roles. When the elements
of sun, wind, and clouds become animate and willful,
nature is rendered close to conspiratorial. A cause-
effect relationship is established between nature,
which here functions as a unit, and Clement. When
Clement's foot touches shore, nature responds with a
kaleidoscope of movement.

It is only after this cause-effect relationship
between natural and human life is established that it
can be inverted in a later passage. Here, it is the
movement of natural elements that causes a reaction in
the robber band.

... When the moon went sailing
like a boat through the heavens,
between long radiant clouds, all
lunar sand bars lying in the
stream, and the stars like little
fishes nibbled at the night, then
it was time for the bandits to ride
home. (p. 83)

The relationship, both in its initial and inverted
states, indicates a link between character and setting,
as if each were not only animate but also dependent
upon the other. Interdependence thus becomes a way of

11

measuring time in the story: the triggering of movement triggers time. When Rosamond's hand touches it,
the gate springs open; when the moon sails through the
heavens, the robbers return. We are aware of time
passing but not of time itself. Time disappears in
action, and action assumes the air of enchantment.

Several passages in the tale show nature in motion
seemingly without cause. The forest has a very
definite life of its own, and can assume a benign or a
malevolent countenance. Early in the tale, for
example, Rosamond exists in a relationship to the
forest that is reminiscent of Snow White's. For her,
the woods are filled with beauty rather than danger.

> How beautiful it was in the
> wild woods! Black willow, green
> willow, cypress, pecan, katalpa,
> magnolia, persimmon, peach, dog-
> wood, wild plum, wild cherry,
> pomegranate, palmetto, mimosa, and
> tulip trees were growing on every
> side, golden-green in the deep
> last days of the Summer. Up over-
> head the cuckoo sang. A quail with
> her young walked fat as the queen
> across the tangled path. A flock
> of cardinals flew up like a fan
> opening out from the holly bush.
> The fox looked out from his hole
> (p. 77)

The description comes close to anthropomorphizing
animal and plant life, which in turn seem to be self-
consciously creating a setting for Rosamond. Nature
appears to intuit Rosamond's innate goodness, reflected in her beauty, and responds with a goodness and
beauty of its own. Clement's innocence is similarly
recognized by nature which, in the form of a willful
willow tree, engages him in mock battle. The pervasive
sound of Indian drums is even perceived and responded
to by the forest itself. In all of these episodes,
nature is capable of incongruous action. Not only do
the leaves chatter the sound of the Indian drums, but
the branches disentangle themselves to reveal Indian
faces, as if both trees and Indians were intent on
observation. It is this sense of the natural environment as aiding or hindering various characters that
lends Welty's tale its most general and overriding
sense of enchantment.

The flying cow of Mobile mentioned above alludes
to yet another folkloristic element -- the use of
ballad as a structural and thematic device. The cow
that jumped over the moon is doubtless the nursery
rhyme echo behind Welty's flying cow. In the locket,
Rosamond's song, and the raven's chant, ballad refrain
suggests Eliade's meaningful repetition. The locket,
for example, is introduced early in the tale as never
failing to produce the statement "If your mother could
see you now, her heart would break" (p. 34) a statement adapted from the original Grimm tale.[22] In its
ability to speak, the locket is magical; through its
placement in the narrative, it is structural and thematic. As a structural leitmotif, the locket emphasizes
Rosamond's plight. It first appears when Rosamond,
sent to fetch herbs by her wicked stepmother, is
walking through a locust grove. She returns safely,
but her next trip through the grove leads to the loss
of her new dress. In a way, the locket verbalizes
Rosamond's lament for the cruelty of her stepmother and
the unfairness of her fate. But if the locket articulates this point of view, it also acts as a talisman
"which kept her from the extravagant harms of the world
and only let her in for the little ones" (p. 45). The
"little harm" that is couched within the locket's
refrain is the loss of clothing, properly lamented, but
only for a moment, three pages later.

After this episode, the locket drops out of the
narrative until, in the middle of the second chapter,
it is stolen by Salome. As soon as the locket is
taken, Rosamond is free. She is led, almost magically,
into the woods, where, equally magically, Jamie appears
and carries her off. The spell continues into the next
chapter, when Rosamond finds Jamie in the woods and
they enter the timeless, placeless cottage.

> If her dead mother could have
> seen Rosamond then, she would
> never have troubled herself to
> come back one more time from the
> repose of Heaven to console and
> protect her, and could have fully
> given herself over to the joys of
> Paradise from then on; that is, if
> she could overlook from that place
> the fact that Jamie was a bandit;
> for Rosamond had quite forgotten
> the locket. (p. 88)

It is not insignificant that the larger "harm" that befalls Rosamond in this second meeting occurs without either locket or refrain. With the disappearance of the locket, Rosamond becomes careless and trusting. She no longer laments her fate and fails to see danger in the forest. Her point of view has altered from cautious to fearless, and only returns to the former with the reappearance of the locket in chapter 4 (p. 127). In viewing the structural placement of these episodes, we can reach the thematic conclusion that the locket literally "sees" only the robber in Jamie, while Rosamond sees only the bridegroom. After Jamie's identity is discovered and he becomes a gentleman, the locket drops out of the story permanently, the point of view which it represented having lost its validity.

Like the locket, Rosamond's song has a definite structural purpose and a thematic significance. The song is a love ballad that recounts the reunion of a woman and her lover.[23] As such, it prefigures much of the action of The Robber Bridegroom. Rosamond and her lover meet and are separated at least twice in the course of the narrative. Given at length this early in the tale, the song identifies Rosamond with the theme of a love quest. The next time she sings it, the song literally produces her lover.

> When he heard Rosamond
> singing so sweetly as if she had
> been practicing just for this, he
> had to look up, and as soon as he
> saw her he turned his horse
> straight up the bank and took it in
> three leaps. (pp. 45-46)

Later, when Rosamond is required to tell Clement the circumstances in which her dress was lost, she begins with the song (p. 52). Although the effect is comic, the repetition strengthens the association between song and lover. As in opera, the refrain here begins to identify the lovers, so that when Goat sings the complete ballad to Rosamond early in chapter 5 (p. 137), the repetition literally voices the tale's happy ending. Meaningful repetition has become the medium through which knowledge is transmitted.

The raven's chant is a leitmotif borrowed from Grimm's "The Robber Bridegroom."[24] As in Grimm's tale, the motif is both structural and thematic in Welty's adaptation. In both tales the raven warns a young

14

woman not to enter an empty cottage in the woods. Welty complicates the original tale, however, in that the raven's chant recurs again and again in the narrative. The bird is introduced in chapter 1 as belonging to Mike Fink, whose intention to rob Clement Musgrove at the inn is forewarned in the refrain "Turn back, my bonny, Turn away home" (p. 6). The irony of this passage is twofold. First, Clement, who has so carefully chosen an honest innkeeper, spends the night in the company of two of the most feared bandits on the Natchez Trace. Second, the raven's warning, no matter how clear and straightforward, is regarded by Clement with total ignorance and innocence.

With Jamie's outwitting of Mike Fink comes ownership of the raven, which is soon established in the robber's wilderness cottage. The events at the cottage in chapters three and four roughly parallel Grimm's tale: a woman enters a deserted cottage despite the raven's warning, witnesses a murder, and escapes being murdered herself. This basic plot line is complicated in Welty's tale, however, when Goat, who has been following her through the woods, obeys the command to "turn away home" that Rosamond ignores. This chant, like that in chapter one, holds a twofold irony. Not only is it ignored by Rosamond, but Rosamond's ignorance is stressed in Goat's immediate compliance. With the burning of the cottage, which signifies the dissolution of the robber band, the raven is freed, never to be seen again (p. 148). When its thematic significance as prophet or oracle has ceased to have an object, the raven, like the locket, is written out of the tale.

Welty borrows several motifs aside from the raven's chant from the original "The Robber Bridegroom." Rosamond is not fond of her prospective husband when he presents himself to her father, and her dislike echoes the response of Grimm's miller's daughter. A second maiden, transformed into an Indian in Welty's adaptation, is murdered in both tales, while the first looks on from a hidden position behind a cask or barrel. The victim is given a colored drink prior to the murder (white, red, and yellow, in Grimm; black in Welty) and suffers the loss of her ring finger, which lands on the lap or in the bosom of the heroine. Welty's adaptation of motif both includes, and extends beyond, the original tale. Rosamond's rapport with nature suggests that of Snow White in "Snow White and the Seven Dwarfs," while her wicked stepmother and transformation from drudge to socialite recall

15

"Cinderella." The extent of Welty's reliance on folk motif is illustrative of the contextual presence of the romantic tradition. As Northrop Frye puts it in The Secular Scripture, "in the criticism of romance we are led very quickly from what the individual work says to what the entire convention it belongs to is saying through the work."[25] Thus, Salome's evil eye and Jamie's enchanted dirk, along with countless other motifs, gain their significance from the long line of witches and talismans to which they belong.

The kind of implausibility traditional to folktale is inherent in both the dialogue and action of Welty's The Robber Bridegroom. Two examples will serve to illustrate her use of the folktale as a narrative technique. In the first, Rosamond is captured, sentenced to death, and reprieved by a cake.

> 'Kill her!,' they cried.
> And they were going to kill
> her, but she said, 'Have some
> cake.' (p. 81)

What is striking in this dialogue is the absence of any relation between the robbers' initial decision to kill Rosamond and their amendment to save her. The passage is reminiscent of the folktale precisely in this disjunction. That is, the reader must rely totally on the narrative as presented without speculating on questions of motive or rationale. In Frye's terms, the reader of this type of literature becomes "too spellbound to question the narrative logic."[26] The second example further illustrates this method of narration when, late in the tale, Rosamond informs us that all Jamie's "wild ways had been shed like a skin, and he could not be kinder to her than he was" (p. 183). The passage is a statement of fact. No reason for Jamie's gentlemanlike behavior is given, nor are we encouraged to speculate on his motives. Unlike the realistic narrative, the folktale demands that we read the lines rather than attempting to read between them.

Salome and Rosamond are presented as conventional characters of folktale precisely through this kind of flatness. They are both one-dimensional, and experience no alteration or growth in character. Salome, the wicked stepmother, is constantly associated with cats, claws, and blackness, while Rosamond is the literal golden maiden. In these repeated associations, the characters of Salome and Rosamond come to

16

be identified as the images themselves. In other words, Salome is blackness just as Rosamond is golden - - "for if Rosamond was as beautiful as the day, Salome was as ugly as the night" (p. 33). When we first hear of Salome, for example, we are told that she has the ability to cast long black shadows (p. 25). A few pages later, she stands in the doorway of Rosamond's room "like an old blackbird" (p. 32), and in a third passage, she watches Rosamond in her new dress with a heart that "felt like lead" (p. 37). Even this early in the narrative, Salome is complete blackness: she projects it, epitomizes it, and even feels like it. She fills the very air about her with a doom as tangible as a physical presence (pp. 55, 62). Salome's dominance over Rosamond is stated in the terms of darkness and light (p. 42). Her downfall is her very ignorance of the sun combined with a quest for "golden glitter" (p. 145). It is, significantly, for daring to "throw mud on the face of the sun" that she is sentenced to death in chapter 5 (pp. 160-164).

Just as Salome is pure blackness, so Rosamond is pure gold. Like Jamie, she is both beautiful and "golden-haired." When she returns, naked, from the indigo field, the coat with which Clement covers her douses her "like a light" (p. 51). The control over Rosamond gained by Salome in chapter 4 is similarly expressed in the terms of light/dark imagery. Rosamond, who has distrusted her up to this point in the narrative, comes to see, quite literally, Salome's point of view.

> So Salome drew so close to Rosamond that they could look down the well and see one shadow, and she whispered in her ear, 'There is one way to find out what your husband looks like, and if you want me to tell you: ask me.'
> 'What way is that?' asked Rosamond, for at last she had to know. (pp. 123-124)

The key phrase in this passage is in the description of Rosamond at last seeing blackness as Salome sees it. Like Mike Fink, however, Rosamond is restored to her former glory by the end of the tale, "dressed in a beautiful, rich white gown" (p. 183).

With Clement, Welty's tale steps out of the traditions of the conventional and folkloristic romance. As

17

a round character, Clement embodies both a social
mythology and the complex perspective inherent to
modern fiction. The mythology of the Old South differs
both from classical mythology and folk legend in that
it is founded on sociological and political issues.
Clement's characteristic innocence, fairness, and
benevolence, coupled with his occupation, evoke the
myth of the Southern plantation owner. He disdains
money for money's sake, sees his riches as a manifestation of $_{27}$ God's grace, and cultivates beauty and
manners.[27] The social myth is that of "the good life"
as exemplified in the pre-Civil War Southern aristoc-
racy; the corresponding political myth is the notion
that slavery was not a commercial venture. The ironies
of these myths are neatly handled in the split between
Clement's character and that of his wife and daughter.
When Rosamond returns, naked, from the woods, for
example, Clement's concern is with the state of her
honor, while Salome's is with the fate of the herbs she
had been gathering (p. 51). Clement's response, that
of the Southern Gentleman, is to avenge his daughter's
honor (p. 55). The force of this position, however, is
undercut by Rosamond herself who, when given a choice
between life and "name" by Jamie, opts for the former
without reservation: "...before I would die on the
point of your sword, I would go home naked any day" (p.
50). Her choice is one that places the reality of her
situation above the myth of the Southern Lady and by
implication, of the Southern Gentleman as well.
Although it is Clement who epitomizes the ideals of the
Southern cotton planter, it is Salome who embodies the
reality of running the plantation. Clement's explanation of this relationship is worth quoting at some
length.

> ... 'Clement,' Salome would say,
> 'I want a gig to drive in to
> Rodney.' 'Let us wait another
> year,' said I. 'Nonsense!' So
> there would be a gig. Next,
> 'Clement, I want a row of silver
> dishes to stand on the shelf.'
> 'But my dear wife, how can we be
> sure of the food to go in them?'
> And the merchants, you know, have
> us at their mercy. Nevertheless,
> my next purchase off the Liverpool
> ship was not a new wrought-iron
> plow, but the silver dishes. And
> it did seem that whatever I asked

of the land I planted on, I would
be given, when she told me to ask,
and there was no limit to its
favors. (pp. 27-28)

Clement's innocence only leads to material success when
overruled by Salome's shrewdness. The social and
political notion of a benevolent, non-profit aristoc-
racy is, after all, a myth.

In examining the elements of myth, legend, and
folktale, we have superficially encountered the theme
of doubleness that becomes most explicit in what can be
regarded as the presence of the past.[28] The juxtaposition of medieval and 19th-century Southern traditions noted earlier in terms of stylistics is equally
present when we examine content. When Clement lands,
on the opening page of the tale, having just sold his
tobacco "for a fair price to the king's men," we are in
a feudal setting. The ritual quest for the damsel in
distress, the protective environment of the feudal
manor and corresponding danger of the surrounding
lands, the concern with honor and "name" --all these
echoes are present in Welty's The Robber Bridegroom.
Both fairy tale and 19th-century Southern society are
here evoked and held throughout the tale. Paradoxically, however, it is this compounded sense of place
and time that underscores the placeless, timeless
quality of the märchen. Because the reader is forced
to view her tale though two pervasive screens --
medieval England and the 19th-century South -- (s)he
can see neither one very clearly. What we get through
reading The Robber Bridegroom is thus the evocation,
rather than the statement, of place and time.

Several specific locations operate within these
general screens. The city of New Orleans, for example,
contains elements both of Paradise and of the violent
South of Mississippi legend.

New Orleans was the most
marvelous city in the Spanish
country or anywhere else on the
river. Beauty and vice and every
delight possible to the soul and
body stood hospitably, and usually
together, in every doorway and
beneath every palmetto by day and
lighted torch by night. A shutter
opened, and a flower bloomed. The

19

very atmosphere was nothing but
aerial spice, the very walls were
sugar cane, the very clouds hung
as golden as bananas in the sky.
(p. 182)

The city is both "marvelous" and very real. It
contains equal portions of beauty and vice, and it is
capable of satisfying the soul as well as the body.
This description of New Orleans depends upon duality
for meaning. Jamie and Rosamond are happy, but no
longer exist in the idyll of the wilderness cottage.
Their paradise has been brought into the world of the
Natchez Trace.

The most important location, however, and one that
extends beyond the regional, is "the bluff where deep
down, under the stars, the dark brown wave of the Mississippi was rolling by" (p. 104). This location
partakes of both the past and the present in its significance to Clement as well as Rosamond: "That was the
place where he had found the river and married Salome.
And if he had but known it, that was the place where
Jamie Lockhart had carried his daughter, there under
the meeting trees at the edge" (pp. 104-105). This
location is further complicated when we view the
circumstances surrounding each marriage. For Clement,
the union with Salome was decreed in a "sign" and
therefore is submitted to, lovelessly but uncom-
plainingly. Rosamond's union, on the other hand, is
based entirely on love to the exclusion, as we have
noted, of caution. Here, location comes to signify
"place" as Welty defines it in her essay "Place in
Fiction." For her, place is inextricably connected
both to feelings and identity. As she puts it at one
point in the essay, "sense of place gives equilibrium;
extended, it is sense of direction, too."[29] The town
of Harpe's Head is a perfect example of this relationship because the name evokes both the identity of Big
Harpe and the legends surrounding his life and death.
It is this sense of place as manifested in identity
that Welty is evoking in the passage quoted above and
in The Robber Bridegroom as a whole. It is the turf on
which meaningful repetition is acted out; it is the
arena that myth, legend, folktale, and regional
mythology conspire to create. Welty's landscape, like
the Impressionist paintings she recalls in her essay,
brings "the mystery of place onto canvas."[30]

With the introduction of character into place,
doubleness becomes a source of conflict and anguish.

20

In Clement's dream, the conflict is defined in terms of
the past and the present.

> 'In the dream, whenever I lie
> down, then it is the past. When I
> climb to my feet, then it is the
> present. And I keep up a struggle
> not to fall.' (p. 29)

The dream functions as a metaphor for Clement's philosophy of duality. As Charles C. Clark has noted,
Clement accepts the connection between good and evil
and realizes the fact that evil can bring about "a
higher happiness than would have been possible without
the evil."[31] Clement's speech on duality late in the
tale echoes this dream of past and present through an
attitude toward fate that is not unlike the medieval
concept of the wheel of fortune.

> ... For all things are double,
> and this should keep us from
> taking liberties with the outside
> world, and acting too quickly to
> finish things off. All things are
> divided in half -- night and day,
> the soul and body, and sorrow and
> joy and youth and age, and some-
> times I wonder if even my own wife
> has not been the one person all the
> time, and I loved her beauty so
> well at the beginning that it is
> only now that the ugliness has
> struck through to beset me like a
> madness. (p. 126)

Amalie is replaced at the top of the wheel by Salome,
just as good is inevitably replaced by evil. As
Clement knows, Jamie's transformation follows the same
pattern: his robber ways are replaced by his kindness
at the end of the tale, just as evil must be supplanted
by good to complete the circle. Past and present
become a continuum in Welty's tale; they form a cycle
symbolic of eternal return.

The theme of duality is visible in several of the
tale's episodes and characters. The Harps are, in
effect, one menace divided in two, just as Rosamond's
pregnancy must result in the birth of twins at the
close of the tale. Jamie and Clement meet twice at the
inn, while Clement's attempts to rescue Rosamond are

described as a "double failure" (p. 115). Finally, when Jamie is introduced to Rosamond, he is fed two antithetical descriptions of her, neither of which appeals to him. Duality is linked in this passage with point of view, which is the essential core of The Robber Bridegroom. As we have already observed in Welty's use of black and gold, point of view appears imagistically on the surface level of the tale. The failure of Jamie and Rosamond to recognize one another typifies this kind of connection between image and meaning. When he applies the berry juice, Jamie becomes the robber that the juice signifies. Similarly, when he visits Clement and meets his daughter, Jamie becomes the man of business, that is, he adopts "business" as a point of view, to such an extent that he does not recognize Rosamond as his lover when he sees her.

> So then Jamie saw Rosamond and they never recognized each other in the world, for the tables were turned; this time he was too clean and she was too dirty. (p. 68)

This reversal signifies nothing but a reversal in point of view. Jamie's mind is on business; Rosamond's is on the robber-bridegroom she imagines to be in the woods. This initial failure of recognition is underscored in the revelation scene toward the close of the tale, when Rosamond removes the berry juice and both she and Jamie see with an expanded point of view.

> Jamie Lockhart opened his eyes and looked at her. The candle gave one long beam of light, which traveled between their two faces.
> 'You are Jamie Lockhart!' she said. 'And you are Clement Musgrove's silly daughter!' said he. (p. 134)

The beam of light that travels between their faces is, quite literally, the beam of knowledge and recognition.

The ability to recognize this kind of paradox is the capacity to perceive and hold a dual point of view. Clement's facility to see complexity in character is part of this modern perspective. Aside from Salome, whose perceptions are part of her characteristic

22

cunning, Clement is the only character capable of
analysis. His lengthy description of "the time of cunning" (pp. 141-144) signifies a thorough understanding
of the disingenuous seen clearly by an ingenuous man.
The recurrence of twos in the description stresses this
dual perspective: Clement speculates on "the time and
the place," he sees two ripples in the Mississippi
followed by a pair of alligator eyes; wrath and love,
the traveler and the bandit, two floors of leaves, loss
and death, heat and cold -- all are recognized by
Clement in this passage. By the end of the tale,
Rosamond and Jamie come to recognize, if not accept,
the paradox of duality. It is only when captured late
in the tale that Rosamond reflects upon the uselessness
of names. The passage echoes back to the discussion of
honor between Rosamond and Clement in chapter 2.

> 'Now that I know his name is
> Jamie Lockhart, what has the news
> brought me?' she asked, and had
> only to look down at the ropes that
> bound her to see that names were
> nothing and untied no knots. (p.
> 150)

Jamie's identity, like Rosamond's honor, is a complex
problem that cannot be adequately untied or resolved by
the name assigned to it. What does untie knots is the
acceptance of conflict and anguish experienced, as
Clement experiences it, in the resolve of two points of
view into a single frame. Perhaps Jamie, who has been
living two lives throughout the tale, expresses it best
when, on its last pages, he senses that identity, point
of view, and a sense of place are merely different
words for the same mystery.

> Then the yellow-haired Jamie
> ran and took him by the hand, and
> for the first time thanked him for
> his daughter. And as for him, the
> outward transfer from bandit to
> merchant had been almost too easy
> to count it a change at all, and he
> was enjoying all the same success
> he had ever had. But now, in his
> heart Jamie knew that he was a hero
> and had always been one, only with
> the power to look both ways and to
> see a thing from all sides. (pp.
> 184-185)

There is an element of irony in the ease with which Jamie transforms himself from bandit to merchant that is not at odds with the notion of regional mythology developed above. It is only after shedding his connection to the Natchez Trace, however, that Jamie Lockhart can become the conventional romantic hero.

In honing Jamie into this final category, Welty is able to transcend, while remaining within, the boundaries of both Southern and romance traditions. What she accomplishes in her tale is the resolve of two literary points of view into a single frame. She has written a romance, but peopled it with a mythic, legendary, and folkloristic population. The conjunction is perhaps the most successful in the twentieth century: The Robber Bridegroom may well be the purest form of Southern Romance to date.

NOTES

[1] In her *Fairy Tale of the Natchez Trace* (Jackson Mississippi Historical Society, 1975), Eudora Welty refers to *The Robber Bridegroom* as a historical novel, but "not a historical historical novel" (p. 9).

[2] John Peale Bishop, "The Violent Country: The Robber Bridegroom," in *The Collected Essays of John Peale Bishop*, ed. Edmund Wilson (New York: Scribner's, 1948), pp. 257-259.

[3] Hoffman defines the tall tale, in his *Form and Fable in American Fiction*, as one of the strands of American Folklore. In this study, the term will follow Stith Thompson's definition of "local legend": "This form of tale purports to be an account of an extraordinary happening believed to have actually occurred." Stith Thompson, *The Folktale* (New York: The Dryden Press, 1951), p. 8.

[4] See, for example, Charles C. Clark, "*The Robber Bridegroom*: Realism and Fantasy on the Natchez Trace," *Mississippi Quarterly*, Vol. xxvi (Fall, 1973), pp. 625-638.

[5] This legend is noted by Alexander Karanikas (*Tillers of a Myth: Southern Agrarians as Social and Literary Critics*. Madison: University of Wisconsin Press, 1966): "Legend: Only the theory of Negro slavery was monstrous; its practice was usually humane. Not addicted to money and commerce, the Southern gentleman could afford to be just and kind to his slaves. It was tragic that his nobility should be replaced by bourgeois avarice and vulgarity" (p. 61).

[6] As Thompson defines it, the märchen is "a tale of some length involving a succession of motifs or episodes. It moves in an unreal world without definite locality or definite characters and is filled with the marvelous." *The Folktale*, p. 8.

[7] Throughout this study, I will be following J. R. R. Tolkien's distinction between "enchantment" and "magic" in his *Tree and Leaf* (Boston: Houghton Mifflin, 1965), pp. 52-53: "Enchantment produces a Secondary World into which both designer and spectator can enter, to the satisfaction of their senses while they are inside, but in its purity it is artistic in

desire and purpose. Magic produces, or pretends to produce, an alteration in the Primary World."

[8]Eudora Welty, The Robber Bridegroom (New York: Atheneum, 1963), p. 63. Subsequent references to this text will be included parenthetically after the quotation.

[9]See "Cupid and Psyche" in Edith Hamilton's Mythology (New York: New American Library, 1940), pp. 92-100.

[10]See The Folktale, pp. 100-101.

[11]See Ashley Brown's analysis of The Robber Bridegroom in relation to Northrop Frye's concept of romance as presented in The Anatomy of Criticism, "Eudora Welty and the Mythos of Summer" (Shenandoah, 20, Spring 1969), pp. 29-35.

[12]Ironically, the "night world" as Frye defines it in The Secular Scripture: A Study of the Structure of Romance (Cambridge: Harvard University Press, 1976) is here the idyll.

[13]Cosmos and History: The Myth of the Eternal Return (New York: Harper and Row, 1954), p. 89.

[14]Ibid., p. 90.

[15]Ibid., pp. 12-17.

[16]The American Adam: Innocence, Tragedy and Tradition in the Nineteenth Century (Chicago: Phoenix Press, 1955), pp. 90-91.

[17]The Outlaw Years: The History of the Land Pirates of the Natchez Trace (New York: Macaulay, 1930), p. 51.

[18]See "Hare," The Outlaw Years (New York: Macaulay, 1930), pp. 73-105.

[19]"The Robber Bridegroom: Realism and Fantasy on the Natchez Trace," pp. 636-637.

[20]See The Robber Bridegroom (New York: Atheneum, 1963), p. 155, and The Outlaw Years (New York: Macaulay, 1930), p. 51.

[21]In her Journal of a Residence on a Georgia Plantation in 1838-1839 (Chicago: Afro-Am Press, 1969), Frances Anne Kemble describes the following condition as typical in a duel: "...whoever kills the other is to have the privilege of cutting off his head and sticking it up on a pole on the piece of land which was the origin of the debate." p. 250.

[22]See also "The Goosegirl" (The Twelve Dancing Princesses and Other Fairy Tales, eds. Alfred David and Mary Elizabeth Meek), p. 33:
"O Young Princess there you go by,
If your mother knew this,
It would break her heart."
This statement is uttered by the head of a talking horse, stuck on a pole.

[23]In "Initiation in Eudora Welty's The Robber Bridegroom" (Southern Humanities Review, 7, Winter 1973), Gordon E. Slethaug identifies this ballad as "Young Andrew" (pp. 80-81).

[24]In the original tale, the chant appears as follows: "Turn back, turn back, young maiden dear, /'Tis a murderer's house you enter here." Joseph Campbell, ed., The Complete Grimm's Fairy Tales, trans., Margaret Hunt (New York: Pantheon Books, 1944), p. 201.

[25]Northrop Frye, The Secular Scripture: A Study of the Structure of Romance (Cambridge: Harvard University Press, 1976), p. 60.

[26]Ibid., p.51.

[27]See Alexander Karanikas, Tillers of Myth: Southern Agrarians as Social and Literary Critics (Madison: University of Wisconsin Press, 1966), p. 60.

[28]Welty discusses the doubleness of the tale in her Fairy Tale of the Natchez Trace (Jackson: Mississippi Historical Society, 1975). For a list of critics who treat doubleness as a motif see Gordon E. Slethaug, "Initiation in Eudora Welty's The Robber Bridegroom" (Southern Humanities Review, 7, Winter 1973), p. 87, footnote 2.

[29]Eudora Welty, "Place in Fiction," in The Eye of the Story (New York: Random House, 1978), pp. 128-129.

[30]Ibid., p. 118.

[31]"The Robber Bridegroom: Realism   and
Fantasy on the Natchez Trace," p. 631.

CHAPTER II. - DELTA WEDDING

With Delta Wedding, Eudora Welty's novels self-
consciously shifted into the twentieth century. That
the transition was not an easy one is evident in the
critical debate surrounding the novel's publication in
1946. Early reviewers of the book, most notably Diana
Trilling and John Crowe Ransom, criticized Delta
Wedding for its failure to address itself to the racial
issues inherent to the South in the early 1940s, the
years during which it was written. Subsequent
reviewers have disagreed with the charges of Trilling
and Ransom, who essentially dismissed the novel as a
celebration of "the narcissistic Southern fantasy" and
"one of the last novels in the tradition of the Old
South."[1] That the novel is, to a certain extent, both
the celebration of a "fantasy" and a narrative in the
Southern tradition cannot be denied. The perspective
of Delta Wedding is, however, much wider than early
critics have allowed. As in each of her novels, Welty
compounds the time and place of Delta Wedding by
establishing limitations on the one hand and obscuring
them on the other. In other words, it is by locating
the novel within time that she frees it from time. In
Eudora Welty, Ruth M. Vande Kieft clarifies Welty's
sense of the way in which time serves Delta Wedding.

> She used the date, after some pre-
> liminary research, as the only
> year in which there had not been,
> either in the world at large or
> that region in particular, some
> external catastrophe such as a
> war, a depression, or a flood. ...
> Miss Welty lifted a particular
> place and time out of history in
> order to learn what might be con-
> tinuing and permanent in human
> relations.[2]

Paradoxically, pinpointing one year in the twentieth
century (1923) became for Welty a means of addressing
the potentiality rather than the actuality of time in
much the same way that focusing on a single location
(the Natchez Trace) had widened the narrative possibilities of place in The Robber Bridegroom.[3]

Both novels begin with the arrival of a central
character, and in each, the stopping place is the land

29

of enchantment. Unlike that of The Robber Bridegroom,
however, which begins with the language of the German
märchen, the narrative starting place in Delta Wedding
is journalism.

> ... The nickname of the train was
> the Yellow Dog. Its real name was
> the Yazoo-Delta. It was a mixed
> train. The day was the 10th of
> September 1923 - afternoon. Laura
> McRaven, who was nine years old,
> was on her first journey alone.[4]

Stylistically, it is the objective world of reportage
(the Primary World, to use J.R.R. Tolkien's terms)[5]
within which the subjective world of the Delta (the
enchanted or Secondary World) is encountered.

> And then, as if a hand reached
> along the green ridge and all of a
> sudden pulled down with a sweep,
> like a scoop in the bin, the hill
> and every tree in the world and
> left cotton fields, the Delta
> began. The drummer with a groan
> sank into sleep. (p. 4)

Delta Wedding is thus fixed, as is The Robber Bridegroom, within specific quadrants of a time-space grid
that is itself infused with mystery.[6] The stylistic
and thematic effect in Delta Wedding is twofold,
serving not only to emphasize the doubleness of the
Delta as a place within a place (a region within Mississippi), but also to signal a transition from the
unenchanted to the enchanted. If the reader sinks into
Laura McRaven's consciousness as dreamily as the drum-
mer sinks into sleep, it is because both are stimulated
by entry into the enchanted landscape of the Delta.

The Delta is, in fact, a landscape located in
romance. In his Custom House introduction to The
Scarlet Letter, Hawthorne suggests that romance
depends, in part, on treatment of subject rather than
choice of subject.[7] Romance, according to Hawthorne,
relies upon the interpenetration of the objective (the
Actual) and the subjective (the Imaginary). While the
Actual establishes parameters (in this case, the
boundaries of the Delta), the Imaginary illuminates
what happens within them. Therefore, the Imaginary is
not event per se, but the interpretation of event by

the observer. Romance is thus the product both of place and of the subjective version of what happens within it. Two images from <u>Delta Wedding</u> will serve both to illustrate this notion of the nature of romance and to establish it as a frame of reference within the novel. The first comes early in the narrative and is given from Laura's point of view.

> Down low over the dinner table hung a lamp with a rectangular shade of tinted glass, like a 'choo-choo boat' with its colored paper windows. In its light she would look over the room, at the youngest ones intertwining on the rug and hating so the approach of night ... -- and it would be as if she had never before seen anything at all of this room with the big breasting china closets and the fruit and cake plates around the rail, had never watered the plants in the window, or encountered till now these absorbed, intent people -- ever before in her life, Laura thought. (p. 21)

The passage illustrates Hawthorne's dictum in that what is being perceived and the manner in which it is observed mingle to create a dissimilar third partaking of both. In Welty's passage, the "rectangular shade of tinted glass" is as much a transforming lens as the windows of the "choo-choo boat" described elsewhere by Welty as "homemade out of every new shoebox, with a candle in the bottom lighted and shining through colored tissue paper pasted over windows scissored out in shapes of the sun, moon, and stars."[8] In both, the colored filter depends upon illumination to alter what is perceived.

The more perfect combination of the Actual and the Imaginary is the china night light given Dabney by Aunts Jim Allen and Primrose.

> The picture on it was a little town. Next, in the translucence, over the little town with trees, towers, people, windowed houses, and a bridge, over the clouds and stars and moon and sun, you saw

> redness glow and the little town
> was all on fire, even to the motion
> of fire, which came from the
> candle flame drawing. (p. 46)

Without illumination, the scene is a static portrait of
London; without the painted shade, the Great Fire of
London is merely candlelight. Candle and scene must be
viewed in conjunction in order to produce the effect of
the Great Fire. In her essay "Place in Fiction," Welty
describes the effect of the night light as one of
"enchantment" dependent upon "the combination of
internal and external, glowing at the imagination as
one."[9] Throughout the novel, the night light carries
an association with the romantic Fairchild past. When
it is given to Dabney, for example, Aunt Primrose
refers to it as "company as early as I can remember --
when Papa and Mama died" (p. 44), and to India it is
filled with the mysteries of time and place (p. 49).
Similarly, after it has been carelessly broken both
India (p. 53) and Dabney (pp. 191-3) feel that something far greater has been lost, and the tone of reconciliation with which the novel ends owes something to
the family's acceptance of this sense of loss.

If the Delta is an enchanted landscape <u>perceived</u>
<u>by</u> the observer, it is also a mindscape -- a region in
which time and place are <u>functions of</u> the observer. In
the Fairchild household, as in that of the Compsons in
<u>The Sound and the Fury</u>, clocks continually strike the
incorrect hour. Objective, or clock time is therefore
dependent upon an act of translation by the viewer.

> 'Your flower girl,' Aunt Tempe
> announced a little later at the
> door of the parlor, where the
> family were gathering for the
> rehearsal supper party -- the
> clock was striking one, which
> meant seven -- 'has the chicken
> pox -- unmistakably. She is con-
> fined to my room.' (p. 180)[10]

Time is neither recorded nor remembered as duration,
but rather as event. In the excerpt quoted above, for
example, time (the striking of the hour) literally
punctuates Aunt Tempe's announcement. The awareness of
time is made synchronous with the relation of event
(the recording of the flower girl's illness) and is
only important within that context. It is this process

32

of viewing time as event that allows the Fairchilds to
lose track of the days of the week when event has not
infused them with significance,[11] while remembering
them vividly when it has. Clearly, the subjective
recording of time is one of the distinctive qualities
of the Fairchilds. As Laura puts it:

> All they remembered and told her
> about was likely to be before
> Laura was born, and they could say
> so easily, 'Before -- or after --
> Annie Laurie died ...,' to count
> the time of a dress being made or a
> fruit tree planted. (p. 134)

The subjective recording of time in relation to event
is, by definition, solipsistic. Obviously, telling
time by the date of Annie Laurie's death will only have
meaning for those who knew, or knew of, Annie Laurie.
An understanding of time therefore presupposes, to a
certain extent, an understanding of family history.

On perhaps its broadest level, Delta Wedding is a
novel about the ways in which individual family members
interpret their collective history. Through inter-
preting their own and each other's actions, the
Fairchild family has turned its history into its story.
Taken as a whole, as interpreted, or translated by its
participants, Fairchild history is a mythology.[12] The
strongest, and most widely endorsed legend within that
mythology is "happiness."[13]

> Passionate, sensitive, to the
> point of strain and secrecy, their
> legend was happiness. 'The
> Fairchilds are the happiest
> people!' They themselves repeated
> it to each other. (p. 222)

The Fairchild legend is, in a sense, an outline of "how
to be." It is a code of conduct based on a family's
perception of itself, a description of what it means to
be a Fairchild. Laura both realizes the existence of
the code and attempts to decipher it the day of her
arrival.

> Things waited for them to appear,
> laughing to one another and
> amazed, in order to happen. They
> were forever, by luck or intui-

33

> tion, opening doors, discovering
> things, little or cherished
> things, running pell-mell down the
> stairs to meet people, ready to
> depart for vague and spontaneous
> occasions. Though everything came
> to Shellmound to them. (p. 15)

Her perceptions are important since she has the
ambiguous position of seeing the Fairchilds from the
point of view of an outsider as well as that of a relation. In the passage quoted above, for example, Laura
senses both the connection between time and event
("things waited for them to appear ... in order to
happen"), and the importance of Shellmound as the locus
of the Fairchild mythology ("everything came to Shellmound to them"). Because of her ambivalent relationship to the family, however, Laura also sees that the
legend of Fairchild happiness is itself double-edged
because "the cousins were a clan. They all said things
and they all kissed one another and yet they all had
secret despiting ways to happiness" (p. 74). It is
the recognition and acceptance of the paradoxes
inherent to the legend that are significant in Laura's
perceptions, as the essence of Shellmound, and the
existence of the Fairchilds within it, is one of
doubleness and ambiguity.

Aunt Shannon illustrates this doubleness through
antithetical traits which surface alternately in an
almost cyclic pattern (p. 63). She also perpetuates
Fairchild mythology by moving freely between past and
present. Early in the novel, for example, Great-Aunt
Shannon is introduced as the aunt

> ... who would talk conversation-
> ally with Uncle Denis and Aunt
> Rowena and Great-Uncle George, who
> had all died no telling how long
> ago, that she thought were at the
> table with her. (p. 13)

Aunt Shannon, like the singers of the early Icelandic
sagas, belongs to the tradition of oral narrative that
views story-telling as performance.[14] What surfaces in
the segments of her dialogue that Welty allows us are
the articulated portions of an integrated, although
primarily soundless, objective oral narration.[15] It is
as if Aunt Shannon were living two separate but con-
gruent lives in much the same way that a schizophrenic

34

lives interconnected but disparate lives.[16] The portions of dialogue that emerge from the non-verbal past life appear unstructured because the rest of the chronicle has progressed soundlessly. Yet Aunt Shannon's chronicle is integrated, as can be seen late in the novel, when Battle attempts to soothe her by adopting the identity of the long-dead Denis.

> She nodded her head, gently and then sharply, and regarded him; India leaned in the door. 'My little old boy,' she said, and patted him. 'Oh, you have a great deal to learn. Oh, Denis, I wish you wouldn't go out in the world unshielded and unprotected as you are. I have a feeling, I have a feeling, something will happen to you ...'
> 'If it isn't the Reconstruction, it's things just as full of trouble to you, isn't it?' Battle said softly, letting her pat her little hand on his great weight, holding still. He changed the level of his voice. 'I'll stay, Aunt Shannon. I'll stay. I'm here. Here I am.'
> 'Good-bye, my darling,' she said. (p. 238)

Aunt Shannon will not allow Battle to rewrite her conversation with Denis because the conversation is part of a much larger construct -- Aunt Shannon's translation of Fairchild history.

Although Aunt Shannon is alone in living a double life in which past and present are superimposed, the remaining Fairchild aunts share her guardianship of history. It is the aunts who perpetuate the Fairchild sense of time as event that so frustrates Laura McRaven in the passage quoted earlier (p. 134). In a sense, the aunts are the time-keepers because they record event. This process is established early in the novel, when Laura first arrives at Shellmound.

> They (the cousins) were never too busy for anything, they were generously and almost seriously of the moment: the past (even

35

Laura's arrival today was past
now) was a private, dull matter
that would be forgotten except by
aunts. (p. 15)

Laura's arrival, like Annie Laurie's death, marks time.
Thus, "before -- or after -- Laura arrived" can potentially become a unit of measurement in the collective
history of the Fairchilds as soon as the event has
occurred. It is the confusion of these units that
irritates Aunts Jim Allen and Primrose when Dabney and
India pay their visit (p. 45) because ghosts, kinfolks,
and tragedies are the components of family history and,
as such, must be held in place in order to maintain the
integrity of the mythology into which they are woven.

Aunt Mac's version of the past is much more active
than those of either her sister, Aunt Shannon, or Aunts
Jim Allen and Primrose, because she is willing to
repeat it in the present (p. 67). Aunt Mac and Aunt
Tempe are opposite poles in the range of Fairchild
aunts, for Tempe is as anxious to obliterate the past
(it is she who thinks Shellmound "outdated", p. 97) as
Mac is capable of reliving it. Both attitudes indicate
an understanding of the way in which past and future
overlap. In order to arrive at this understanding, it
will first be necessary to define "past" and "future,"
and physics is as good a place as any to find definitions. In his Physics and Philosophy, Werner
Heisenberg defines the terms as follows:

When we use the term 'past' we
comprise all those events which we
could know at least in principle,
about which we could have heard at
least in principle. In a similar
manner we comprise by the term
'future' all those events which we
could try to change or to prevent
at least in principle.[17]

According to Heisenberg's definitions, the Fairchild
aunts can be said to believe that both future events
can be known and past events altered by the present.
In other words, to borrow from T.S. Eliot,

Time present and time past
Are both perhaps present in time
future,
And time future contained in time
past.

36

> If all time is eternally present
> All time is unredeemable.[18]

This understanding of the interdependence between past
and future is best seen in a description of the library
at Shellmound given early in the novel.

> Even from the door, the library
> smelled of a tremendous dictionary
> that had come through high water
> and fire in Port Gibson and had now
> been left open on a stand, proba-
> bly by Shelley. On the long wall,
> above the piles of bookcases and
> darker than the dark-stained
> books, was a painting of Great-
> Great-Uncle Battle, whose name was
> written in the flyleaf of the
> dictionary. It was done from
> memory by his brother, Great-
> Grandfather George Fairchild, a
> tall up-and-down picture on a slab
> of walnut, showing him on his
> horse with his saddle bags and
> pistols, pausing on a dark path
> between high banks, smiling not
> down at people but straight out
> into the room, his light hair gone
> dark as pressed wildflowers. His
> little black dogs, that he loved
> as a little boy, Great-Grand-
> father had put in too. Did he look
> as if he would be murdered? Cer-
> tainly he did, and he was. Side by
> side with Old Battle's picture was
> one of the other brother, Denis,
> done by a real painter, change-
> lessly sparkling and fair, though
> he had died in Mexico, 'marching
> on a foreign land.' Behind the
> glass in the bookcase hiding the
> books, and out on the tables, were
> the miniatures in velvet cases
> that opened like little square
> books themselves. Among them were
> Aunt Ellen's poor mother (who had
> married some Lord in England, or
> had died) and the three brothers
> and the husbands of Aunt Mac and
> Aunt Shannon, who could not be

told apart. from one another by the
children; but no matter what hide-
and-seek went on here, in this
room where so many dead young
Fairchilds, ruined people, were,
there seemed to be always consciousness of their gazes, so
courteous and meditative they
were. Coming in, gratefully
bringing out her book, Laura felt
it wordlessly; the animation of
the living generations in the
house had not, even in forgetting
identity, rebuked this gentleness,
because the gentleness was still
there in their own faces, part of
the way they were made, the
nervous, tender, pondering fore-
head, the offered cheek -- the
lonely body, broad shoulder,
slender hand, the long pressing
thigh of Old Battle Fairchild
against his horse Florian. (pp.
54-5)

Aunt Shannon is able to move freely between events of
the past and those of the future because she knows that
they are both as "eternally present" in the portraits[19]
of Denis as they are in the living Fairchilds. Even
Laura can sense a quality (she calls it "gentleness")
in the way all the Fairchilds, both living and dead,
have been made, and perhaps it is this quality that
enables her to predict Great-Grandfather George
Fairchild's death in the portrait of him painted many
years before.

If past and future events can be altered in the
present, then we have not only reached the land[20] of
enchantment, but the land of "potentia" as well. What
Laura sees in the portrait of Great-Grandfather George
Fairchild is, to use Heisenberg's terms, a "tendency
toward something" -- a probability, in this case, that
he will be murdered. This kind of knowledge is strong
enough to constitute a physical reality that is itself
based on a prediction of probability. It is, again to
quote Heisenberg,

... something standing in the mid
dle between the idea of an event
and the actual event, a strange

38

> kind of physical reality just in
> the middle between possibility and
> reality.

The potential of the moment both to reveal and to alter past and future is encountered at every turn in the novel. Laura's belief that "at any moment she might learn everything" (p. 14) is echoed in differing forms by various characters throughout the narrative. It is the feeling that the moment can reveal all, that "in the Delta, all the air everywhere is filled with things -- it's the shining dust that makes it look so bright" (p. 137) that both silences the household during India's act of wishing (p. 27), and presses a knowledge of future laughter or tears into a tranquil morning (p. 54). Similarly, the ability of the moment to alter past and future is felt at different points by George (p. 57), Dabney (p. 220), and Ellen (p. 223), and it is Laura, the outsider, who appears at least once in the novel to understand the legend that at other times mystifies her.

> 'My secret is,' Laura murmured,
> 'I've been in Marmion afore ye.
> I've seen it all afore. It's all
> happened afore.' (p. 241)

That Laura can feel part of the Fairchild past and future is due to the significance it holds in the present.

In his perceptive article, John Edward Hardy discusses the power of the Fairchild legend to infuse objects, people, and other legends with its own significance.[21] Although the Fairchild myth owes this significance to its historians (the Fairchild women), it owes much of its permanence to its subject (the Fairchild men). As Laura realizes early in the novel,

> The boys were only like all the
> Fairchilds, but it was the boys
> and the men that defined that
> family always. All the girls knew
> it. (p. 14)

Throughout the novel, the women observe and define their men in relation to one another, whether through physical differences and similarities (p. 22), or as exhibiting the "Fairchild temper" (p. 106) in its various moods and forms (cf. pp. 103, 161-2). Comparison of this sort inevitably leads to memories of Denis and his significance to the Fairchild myth, for Denis is the ideal Fairchild against which all other Fairchild men are measured. An elusive figure throughout the novel, Denis is the most living of the Fairchild ghosts. His portrait is described above as "changelessly sparkling and fair," and it is to this image that Aunt Shannon addresses her remarks. Even Maureen serves as a constant reminder of Denis and the mysterious choice he made in loving her mother, Virgie Lee. His is the myth of the brave youth tragically killed in battle, and is therefore a myth of lost potential.[22]

The Fairchild forced to adopt and carry the myth as bequeathed by Denis is George. That the two men have been linked in the collective consciousness of both family and town is evident in an incident recalled by Dabney early in the novel (pp. 35-7). The incident, which had involved ending a fight between two slaves, is itself minor. What has rendered it significant is Denis's death the following year. George's life became doubly important to the Fairchilds the moment Denis's ended because it began to be measured not only in terms of what George himself could do (his potential), but also in terms of what Denis could have done (his lost potential).[23] The connection between the two is therefore as profound as it is permanent. What Denis and George are thought to share by the Fairchilds is implicit in Dabney's recollection.

> The other Fairchilds never said but one thing about George and Denis, who were always thought of together -- that George and Denis were born sweet, and that they were not born sweet. Sweetness then could be the visible surface of all the darkness that might frighten her. (p. 37)

What Dabney perceives when she thinks about the ambivalence of George's and Denis's sweetness is the kind of duality in myth that Laura glimpses in the Fairchild legend of happiness. For both women, the interpretation of event leads to a more complete understanding of the myth.

Family myth is sustained, to a large extent, by regional myth, so that the myth of the Fairchilds is

40

both insulated and fed by the myths of the Deltan, the Mississippian, and the Southerner. Throughout the novel, the Delta is viewed as a land of enchantment, a place steeped in memory. Leaving it, or deviating from its code of behavior, are therefore impossible for any right-thinking Deltan. Aunt Tempe's "What will the Delta think?" (p. 243), and Aunt Jim Allen's "It's not as if you were going out of the Delta, of course" (p. 44) are thus refrains indicating a regional limitext within which family myth is to function. As Laura observed upon her arrival at Shellmound,

> ... boys and men, girls and la-
> dies, all, the old and the young of
> the Delta kin -- even the dead and
> the living for Aunt Shannon --were
> alike -- no gap opened between
> them. (p. 14)

Laura's perception of a likeness among Delta kin not only suggests similarity in physical appearance, but also the shared point of view implicit in Aunt Tempe's and Aunt Jim Allen's refrains. It is this unified per-spective that separates the Delta kin from Mississip-pians and other Southerners (p. 95).

The traditions of Fairchild honor and pride,[24] however, belong to the myth of the Southern gentleman plantation owner. Battle Fairchild is lord and master of Shellmound, his wife, and his children. Both imposing and good-natured, he is a horseman, a cotton planter, and a perfect example of Southern hospitality and manners (pp. 11-12). His wife, Ellen, a Virginian, has filled the role expected of her by having eight children (and expecting a tenth; the ninth had died), overseeing the day-to-day needs of the household, and accomodating the influx of guests and relations surrounding Dabney's wedding. Ellen's performance as mistress of Shellmound can perhaps be gauged by that of her mother, who, when Ellen was nine years old, left Virginia for England and a British lover, only returning after three years (p. 157). The incident is significant in the way it is perceived by the Fairchilds, who, in the passage describing the library above, remember her as "Aunt Ellen's mother (who had married some Lord in England, or had died)." Even though the point of view here is Laura's it suggests that of the Southerner for whom relocation to the North is, in effect, a death.[25] Together, therefore, Battle and Ellen comprise the active core of the plantation.

41

The values inherent to Shellmound are those of the South as presented in I'll Take My Stand by twelve Southerners who could have been the contemporaries of Battle Fairchild. Briefly, these values include adherence to religion, support and cultivation of classical education and the arts, pursuit of Agrarianism over Industrialism, and practice of "the social exchanges which reveal and develop sensibility in human affairs" ("manners, conversation, hospitality, sympathy, family life, romantic love").[26] In praising the Southern way of life, the Agrarians are praising a space-time grid within which the Delta is located. That is, if Agrarianism is a point of view, then the idea of the South that it presupposes is composed both of time seen through place and place viewed over time. The Delta is thus a small mindscape within a much larger mindscape (the South) that is itself dependent upon the way in which it is perceived. It is precisely the distance between observer (Fairchild or Agrarian) and object (in this case, region) that makes for mythology. If time is marked by what is significant in event (cf. p. 134), then mythology can be defined as the accumulation of significance through time. In "Some Notes on River Country," Welty writes:

> Whatever is significant and whatever is tragic in its story live as long as the place does, though they are unseen, and the new life will be built upon these things -- regardless of commerce and the way of rivers and roads, and other vagrancies.[27]

It must therefore be Robbie Reid from Fairchilds (the observer farthest removed from the myth of the Southern gentleman plantation owner) who contests the way in which Shellmound is perceived by the Fairchild family.

> 'You're all a spoiled, stuck-up family that thinks nobody else is really in the world! But they are! You're just one plantation with a little crazy girl in the family, and listen at Miss Shannon. You're not even rich! You're just medium. Only four gates to get here, and your house needs a coat of paint! You don't even have one of those little painted wooden

42

niggers to hitch horses to!' (p.
163)

Robbie can respond to Shellmound in this way because
its story holds no significance for her.

Obviously, then, place has much to do with identity. In her essay "Place in Fiction," Welty makes the
association explicit.[28] It is not surprising,
therefore, that a description of Shelley's room (pp.
82-4) is as much a definition of her as anything she
says or does in the novel, and that it is similarly her
own "place" in Memphis that Robbie recalls (pp. 138-40)
as a defense against her return to Shellmound. Neither
is it surprising that the marriage of Robbie and
George, and the upcoming wedding of Dabney and Troy,
are problematic because in each a Fairchild is
marrying, quite literally, out of "place." It is
because Robbie is from Philadelphia and Troy from the
hill country of Mississippi that difficulties arise.
Outsiders to Shellmound, or plantations like
Shellmound within the Delta, simply do not share either
its values or its sense of identity. Quite naturally,
therefore, the question of where the outsider lives
becomes one of who the outsider is (p. 26). Aunt Jim
Allen's reluctance to accept Troy, for example, has
much to do with the incongruities of picturing him at
the Grove.

> 'We've never really seen Troy,'
> Aunt Jim Allen said faintly. She
> did sound actually afraid of Troy.
> 'Not close to -- you know.' She
> indicated the walls of the green-
> lit parlor with her little ringed
> finger. (p. 44)

The fact that Troy is, as even Partheny recognizes,
"low-born" (p. 132) accounts for most of the Fairchild
animosity toward him. Aunt Tempe, for example, dismisses him as "the overseer" (p. 101), Aunt Mac would
just as soon throw him in the bayou (p. 67), and India
sees him as "a black wedge in the lighted window" of
Shellmound (p. 53).

Yet Troy is not the only character whose identity
is reduced to the circumstances of place. Although she
is accepted as a Fairchild, Laura McRaven is as much an
outsider as is Troy. Both are defined by the
Fairchilds according to their reasons for being at

Shellmound. Thus, if Troy is viewed in relation to his position as "the overseer," then Laura is similarly understood in terms of her reason for living at Shellmound -- her mother's death. Throughout the novel, therefore, Laura is viewed as the "poor little motherless girl" who has been given a place.

> When she got there, 'Poor Laura, little motherless girl,' they would all run out and say, for her mother had died in the winter and they had not seen Laura since the funeral. (p. 3)

A formula for viewing Laura is thus established on the first page of the narrative[29] and continues as an unbroken shorthand for her. "Your Aunts" is a similar family shorthand that indicates Aunts Jim Allen and Primrose, the "old-maid" aunts who inhabit the Grove (pp. 28, 40), and is never applied to any of the other Fairchild aunts. The spinsterhood of these two aunts is intimately connected with their life at the Grove, for a description of the house reveals the network of Fairchilds within which the aunts are set, like a detail of Monet's "Water Lilies" -- individual, but belonging to the same family (pp. 40-1).

With the notion of belonging we once again return to Robbie Reid. If the myth of the gentleman plantation owner holds little significance for Robbie, then the myth of the Fairchild family holds even less. Throughout the novel, it is Robbie who is most critical of the egocentricity of the Fairchilds, even though Troy at times feels a similar exclusion from them.

> 'I wanted to turn into a Fairchild. It wasn't that I thought you were so wonderful. And I had a living room for him just like Miss Tempe's. But that isn't what I mean.
> 'But you all -- you don't ever turn into anybody. I think you are already the same as what you love. So you couldn't under- stand. You're just loving your- selves in each other --yourselves over and over again!' (p.165)

For Robbie, family implies both point of view and place. She realizes that she has not become a Fairchild (even though she carries the name, she is still referred to as Robbie Reid by the family), and that she will always be an outsider to Shellmound. It is Aunt Tempe who, late in the novel, articulates the family point of view in analyzing the effects of Robbie and Troy on the Fairchilds.

> 'Well, one thing,' said Tempe in a low voice to Shelley, looking after the fern with a sigh of finality, 'when people marry beneath them, it's the woman that determines what comes. It's the woman that coarsens the man. The man doesn't really do much to the woman, I've observed.
> 'You mean Troy's not as bad for us as Robbie,' whispered Shelley intently.
> 'Exactly!' (pp. 205-6)[30]

The ongoing battle between Robbie and the Fairchilds over George is crucial primarily because George is "the very heart of the family" (p. 33). It is George's identity, therefore, that constitutes whatever is essential to the Fairchild character.

If Denis is the ideal representation of what the Fairchilds might have been, then George is the literal image of what being a Fairchild is. Early in the novel, it is Dabney who perceives him as the heart of the family, but a heart that has a life apart from the body it enlivens. This notion of being central but isolated recurs in the perceptions of him given by other characters in the novel,[31] and it is Robbie who expresses his relationship to the family most clearly.

> George was not the one they all looked at, she thought in that moment, as he was always declared to be, but the eye that saw them, from right in their midst. He was sensitive to all they asked of life itself. Long ago they had seized on that. He was to be all in one their lover and protector and dreaming, forgetful con-science. (p. 212)

Yet, paradoxically, the conscience of the family is the very member who is "driven to detachment" (p. 186) by its indulgence and demands (pp. 161, 191). Paradoxically also, George is the pride of both Shellmound and the Grove even though he lives in Memphis -- he is both the Fairchild who left the Delta for Robbie Reid, and the one who returned to risk his life for the simple-minded Maureen. George is ultimately accused by Robbie of belonging too much to the Fairchilds as well as resented by the family for belonging too much to the world. The incident that spurs both reactions and the event around which much of the novel revolves, is the episode involving Maureen's near-death by the Yellow Dog.

John Edward Hardy has rightly observed that in Delta Wedding "it is not actions, but reactions, which are to count."[32] The Delta, like Faulkner's Mississippi, is a place in which events recur both in fact and in the imagination. As Robbie puts it, "things almost never happened, almost never could be, for one time only! They went back again ... started over ..." (p. 244). Reacting to event implies re-enacting event, and the medium through which event is re-enacted is the story.[33] If George is the center of the Fairchild family circle, then his rescue of Maureen is the central story around which the family circles. Orrin (pp. 19-20), India (pp. 58-61), and Roy (p. 115) all have their turn at telling it to Laura, Mr. Rondo, and Aunt Tempe, while for Shelley (pp. 87-9), Robbie (pp. 141-2), and Ellen (p. 188), the story is invested with a significance that they both try to analyze and attempt to come to terms with. Shelley's recollection illustrates the extent to which the incident has become a preoccupation.

> The scene on the trestle was so familiar as to be almost indelible in Shelley's head, for her memory arrested the action and let her see it with colors vivid and thunderclouded, George and Maureen above locked together, and the others below with the shadow of the trestle on them. (p. 87)

The family is preoccupied with this incident because it in some way captures the essence of George's relationship to himself, his wife, and the Fairchilds. George rescues Maureen because, as both Robbie and

46

Ellen realize, it was inevitable that he should. As the center of the circle, the focal point of the family, George must intercept whatever dangers time and chance bring within them. It is therefore unavoidable that he risk his life for Maureen, just as it is inevitable that he sleep with the mysterious and beautiful girl whom Ellen encounters in the woods (p. 79). In a sense, the circle is completed with this girl, who partakes of George's love as part of a ceremony that had begun with Maureen's rescue and ends in her own death (p. 218).

The circle as a motif is linked throughout the novel with the family circle of the Fairchilds. Early in the narrative, Shellmound is encircled by silvery-blue clouds (p. 30), Aunt Tempe (p. 115) and Mr. Rondo (p. 59) are circled by Lady Clare and Bluet upon their separate arrivals at Shellmound, laughter circles the table at noon dinner (p. 153), Ellen is encircled by Fairchilds when she faints (p. 167), and a circle of listeners forms to hear her story of Shelley's birth (pp. 214-16). Dabney's wedding present from her aunts is a night light (itself circular) that seems to India, as she makes "a circle with her fingers, imagining she held the little lamp," filled with the air of night (p. 49). The house itself is ringed both without and within by servants the day of the wedding (p. 211), and the wedding rehearsal merges with George's and Robbie's reconciliation in a scene entirely constructed in circling patterns.

> In the music room Mary Lamar resumed playing 'Constantinople' and the bridesmaids, rising a little blankly as if from sleep or rest, took the groomsmen and began to dance here in the room, and around George and Robbie there in the center. Aunt Tempe too, with her finger drawing little circles, kept time. While George was kissing Robbie, Bluet had him around his knees and kissed him down there, with such fervor that she sat down, sighing. Then George and Robbie were dancing too -- how amazingly together they went. In and out wove little Ranny, waving a pretended shepherd crook, shouting 'I'm the wedding!'

and stamping the floral wreath in
the rug. (p. 189)

Although primarily associated with reconciliation and
harmony, the circle can indicate chaos and confusion as
well. Dabney, for example, sees an ambiguity in the
way the Fairchilds "took you in circles" (p. 190), and
in analyzing her feelings while engaged in the game "Go
In and Out the Window," Laura comes to an insight about
the ambivalent nature of circles (p. 73).

The ability of the circle to include or exclude
the individual is a metaphorical statement about the
duality inherent to the Fairchild legend. The alter-
nation between wanting to belong to the family circle
and wanting to remain separate accounts for the
disparate ways in which the Fairchilds regard one
another and themselves. Within the circle lie security
and restraint, without are freedom and chaos. A circle
can therefore be as much a trap as a sacred territory.
It can bar from without as well as from within. Again,
it is Laura who understands this early in the novel
when she visualizes the Fairchilds as birds within a
cage.

> ... Laura found herself with a
> picture in her mind of a great
> bowerlike cage full of tropical
> birds her father had shown her in a
> zoo in a city -- the sparkle of
> motion was like a rainbow, while
> it was the very thing that broke
> your heart, for the birds were
> caged all the time and could not
> fly out. (p. 15)

What entraps the Fairchilds is love. If the family is
both entrapped and sustained by Shellmound, then so are
its individual members both caught and nurtured by one
another. One individual must, in a sense, belong to
another in order for that other to understand the
individual in any meaningful way. It is the knowledge
of oneself existing in another, therefore, that is
binding. Love is thus double-edged because it both
frees and enslaves. It is this potential to construct
a cage, or "house within you", that Dabney recognizes
in George.

> She had then known something that
> he knew all along, it seemed, then

48

        -- that when you felt, touched,
heard, looked at things in the
world, and found their fragrances,
they themselves made a house
within you, which filled with life
to hold them, filled with
knowledge all by itself, and all
else, the other way to know,
seemed calculation and tyranny.
(p. 34)

"Other ways to know" are calculated because they are
false. That is, they do not arise out of love.

    In a sense, the "house within you" is reflected
from without because, as we have said, identity
partakes of place. What fills the house is knowledge
viewed through the lens of love. Therefore, it is love
that enlivens. The house at Shellmound is thus viewed,
from the first, as a living organism (p. 6). China
vibrates (p. 17), and objects of every sort tell
stories to Aunt Tempe when she surveys the parlor
quickly, "as if to catch it before it could compose
itself" (p. 97). Like the "house within you", therefore, Shellmound is a storage place of coded event, if
you will -- event that depends upon the observer for
translation. The photograph taken of the wedding party
(p. 217), for example, is event (Dabney's marriage)
frozen and recorded. But the photograph, like the
portraits of Denis hanging in the library, must be
interpreted through a lens, and the lens must partake
of love.

    Love is here a transforming, as well as a life-
giving power. It is what motivates the Fairchilds to
translate event into significance and weave significance over time into mythology. If the medium
through which event is re-enacted is the story, then
the authority of the story-teller, or narrative voice,
is crucial. The attitude of the Fairchilds toward
story-telling is made explicit prior to the first
retelling of the incident involving Maureen and George
on the train trestle. For the children, as for Aunt
Shannon, story-telling is the accurate performance and
transmission of one's own version of history.

        For all of them told happenings
    like narrations, chronological and
    careful, as if the ear of the world

                    listened   and   wished   to   know
                    surely.   (p. 19)

Like Aunt Shannon, the rest of the Fairchilds are
intimately connected with the stories they record and
recite. Shelley's diary entry (pp. 84-6), for example,
reflects not only an understanding of her own history
but also an awareness of the larger history of the
Fairchilds of which it forms a part, just as Ellen's
story of Shelley's birth (pp. 214-16) extends both
backward in time to her mother, and forward in time to
Shelley's perceptions of herself and her position
within the family (p. 229). Not surprisingly, George's
sense of the importance of the story is the greatest,
as he is its living protagonist.

                    He looked out at the world, at her,
                    sometimes, with that essence of
                    the remote, proud, over-innocent
                    Fairchild look that she suspected,
                    as if an old story had taken hold
                    of him -- entered his flesh. And
                    she did not know the story. (p.
                    191)

Love motivates translation of history into story
because the Fairchilds believe that language can order
chaos. That is why Robbie cannot possibly understand
the myth George has become caught within, and why the
Fairchilds circle around event by re-enacting it
through their mythology.

     Ultimately, the need to create a romance springs
from the need to justify a code of conduct, or "how to
be." It is a way of ordering chaos. Obviously,
Shellmound is a place within a place, a mindscape
located within a combination of the Actual and the
Imaginary, and is defined by its inhabitants. What
Shellmound is therefore depends a great deal upon what
its inhabitants say it is. The novel can be seen as a
kind of verbal photograph album, a montage of anecdotes
and myths that freeze character in much the same way as
a photograph would. In the photograph of the wedding
party, Ellen's reverie of her past life as "a town-
loving, book-loving young lady of Mitchem Corners" (p.
217) is erased by the photographer's flash. Who Ellen
could have been is not part of the plantation mistress
recorded in the wedding photograph. Story functions in
the same way. It re-enacts event as perceived by the
family and therefore becomes as static and as incapable

of contradicting the Shellmound code of conduct as the
photograph. After seeing blood on Troy's door, for
example, Shelley begins to question codes of behavior.
The passage is important as it demonstrates the power
of the romance over thought.

> Running back along the bayou,
> faster than she had come, Shelley
> could think in her anger of the
> convincing performance Troy had
> given as an overseer born and
> bred. Suppose a real Deltan, a
> planter, were no more real than
> that. Suppose a real Deltan only
> imitated another Deltan. Suppose
> the behavior of all men were
> actually no more than this --
> imitation of other men. But it had
> previously occurred to her that
> Troy was trying to imitate her
> father. (Suppose her father
> imitated ... oh, not he!) Then all
> men could not know any too well
> what they were doing. Everybody
> always said George was a second
> Denis. (p. 196)

Shelley cannot believe her father to be an imitation
even though she can accept George as a reincarnation of
Denis because, quite simply, "everybody always said" he
was -- that is, the myth supports the point of view.
Significantly, one of the things that distinguishes
Troy from the Fairchilds is the fact that, unlike them,
he is "slow on words" (p. 31) -- e.g., not part of the
myth-making process. What Diana Trilling and John
Crowe Ransom were in fact criticizing in Delta Wedding,
therefore, was the ability of the Fairchilds to create
a romance and live within it. Ultimately, then, Delta
Wedding is a "narcissistic Southern fantasy", but one
belonging exclusively to the Delta Fairchilds as Welty
views them over one week in September of 1923.

NOTES

[1]Diana Trilling, "Fiction in Review." _Nation_, 11 May 1946, p. 578; John Crowe Ransom, "Delta Fiction." _Kenyon Review_, 8 (Summer 1946), p. 507.

[2]Ruth M. Vande Kieft, _Eudora Welty_ (New York: Twayne Publishing Co., 1962), p. 109.

[3]John Edward Hardy, in "_Delta Wedding_ as Region and Symbol," _Sewanee Review_, 60 (July-Sept. 1952), pp. 397-417, believes that by locating her novel in the Twenties, Welty puts "the emphasis just where she wants it, upon probability rather than upon the kind of mere possibility which our own generation demands not only of the immediately contemporary novel, but of the usual historical one as well." (p. 403)

[4]Eudora Welty, _Delta Wedding_ (New York: Harcourt, Brace and Co., 1946), p. 3. Subsequent references to this text will be included parenthetically after the quotation.

[5]J.R.R. Tolkien, _Tree and Leaf_ (Boston: Houghton Mifflin, 1965), pp. 52-3.

[6]This notion will become clearer with the discussion of regional myth below.

[7]Nathaniel Hawthorne, The Custom House preface to _The Scarlet Letter_ (New York: The New American Library, 1959), p. 45.

[8]Eudora Welty, "The Little Store," from _The Eye of the Story_ (New York: Random House, 1978), p. 327.

[9]Eudora Welty, "Place in Fiction," from _The Eye of the Story_, pp. 119-120.

[10]See also p. 20.

[11]See, for example, p. 77 ("There was a feeling in the infinity of the Delta that even the bounded things, waiting, for instance, could go on forever"), and p. 228 ("We have every one lost track of the day of the week").

[12]Throughout this study, I will be following the definition of "mythos" supplied by Robert Scholes and Robert Kellogg in The Nature of Narrative (London: Oxford University Press, 1966), who use the word in its ancient Greek context to mean "a traditional story." (p. 12).

[13]Other, less significant but generally accepted components of the Fairchild myth include intensity (p. 50), an ability to personalize anecdote (p. 56), and a tendency toward self-centeredness (p. 80).

[14]Robert Scholes and Robert Kellogg, The Nature of Narrative, p. 24.

[15]Scholes and Kellogg define objective narrative as told by a narrator who "does not talk about himself, but about the characters and actions of his story. Nor does he cultivate the intimacy of his audience at the expense of their sympathy with the story." The Nature of Narrative, p. 51.

[16]See John Wier Perry, The Far Side of Madness (Englewood Cliffs: Prentice-Hall, 1974), p. 8.

[17]Werner Heisenberg, Physics and Philosophy: The Revolution in Modern Science (New York: Harper & Row, 1958), pp. 114-15.

[18]T.S. Eliot, Four Quartets (New York: Harcourt, Brace & World, Inc., 1943), p. 3.

[19]It is not insignificant, therefore, that Ellen's tenth child will be named Denis Fairchild (p. 241).

[20]Werner Heisenberg, Physics and Philosophy, pp. 40-41, all references.

[21]John Edward Hardy, "Delta Wedding as Region and Symbol," p. 410.

[22]Aunt Tempe, for example, believed that Denis was the most extravagant of the Fairchilds, capable of the spectrum of human possibility. The family's loss is therefore all the greater for, as she says, "Denis could have been anything and done any-thing, but he was cut off before his time" (p. 116).

[23]See, for example, the comments of India and Aunt Tempe, p. 245.

[24]Cf. pp. 120-1, 165, 95, 105.

[25]Aunt Tempe's perception of herself as a failure is typical of this point of view, and it is because her own daughter married a Yankee that she curtails her censorship of Troy Flavin (pp. 100-1). See also pp. 99, 104, 107.

[26]I'll Take My Stand: The South and the Agrarian Tradition, by Twelve Southerners. (New York: Harper and Brothers, 1930), p. xv.

[27]Eudora Welty, "Some Notes on River Country," The Eye of the Story, p. 299.

[28]Eudora Welty, "Place in Fiction," The Eye of the Story, pp. 128-33.

[29]See also pp. 10, 62, 103. It is interesting to note that, like Rosamond of The Robber Bridegroom, Laura McRaven both wears a locket that is a symbol of her lost mother (p. 10) and visualizes her mother's sorrow at Laura's lucklessness (p. 75).

[30]Dabney's understanding of the difference between what it means to be a Fairchild for a man and for a woman comes much earlier in the novel (pp. 32-3).

[31]See, for example, p. 47 (where Dabney sees George as a "solid wall of too much love"), pp. 63-4 (Ellen's meditation on George's uniqueness), p. 75 (Laura's realization that "it was right for him to stand apart"), and p. 157 (Ellen's moment of acknowledging "George single himself from them").

[32]John Edward Hardy, "Delta Wedding, as Region and Symbol," p. 403.

[33]Although I will only be dealing with stories as they pertain to family myth in Delta Wedding, numerous others revolving around superstitions and legends can be traced throughout the novel. Roy's fears of Parchman and the legends it has inspired (pp. 9, 170, 230), various ghost stories (pp. 34, 45, 69, 123, 239), anecdotes defining etymology (pp. 72-3, 194), and stories explaining events as they portend good or bad luck (pp. 142, 159) all serve to

illustrate the Fairchild belief in the power of language to order and re-enact event.

CHAPTER III. - THE PONDER HEART

Like The Robber Bridegroom, The Ponder Heart
sustains a cohesive stylistic and thematic language and
like Delta Wedding, it comprises a signature of location on a space-time grid. The language of the tale is
that of its teller, Miss Edna Earle Ponder, and its
signature is her own. For the story quite literally
takes "place" within Edna Earle's mind, and it is only
through the medium of re-telling that the narrative per
se emerges. Robert B. Holland, in "Dialogue as a
Reflection of Place in The Ponder Heart,"¹ has isolated
the elements of Edna Earle's language to correspond to
the speech patterns of a type of place -- the rural
middle-class Mississippi town. If, as Holland
believes, the style of Edna Earle's language is "a
vocalization of the design of the culture" in which she
moves and suggests the kind of community nexus she
inhabits, then the content of that language focuses the
reader on the particular town she knows -- Clay, Mississippi. The ultimate object of Edna Earle's vision
and the subject of her articulation is, in fact, the
town of Clay only insofar as it contributes to an
understanding of Uncle Daniel Ponder. Edna Earle's
language therefore must reflect a kind of self-editing
process which enables her, like some film directors, to
edit "in camera" (or "in mind," if you will) rather
than after the impression has been taken, so that what
is recorded is itself the subjective, or personal
story.²

If we follow Northrop Frye's definition of myth as
an imitation of ritual (e.g., plot),³ then Edna Earle's
narrative can be seen as an ironic myth, or romance
parody. That is, the events of the story comprise a
quest, but one that recounts events leading to isolation rather than reconciliation, revealed through a
disparity between what the reader comes to know and
what Edna Earle cannot see (that is, what she has
edited from her perceptions). For our purposes, then,
the ironic myth is the distance between what Edna Earle
says and what the reader hears. In order to understand
the latter, it will be necessary to examine the former,
which can be separated into the following elements of
Southern Romance: regional myth surrounding the
Southern character, geographic legend, family myth
(here incorporating a preoccupation with identity in
relation to name), acceptance of the authority of the
narrative voice, repetition of incident, belief in the

ability of language to order chaos, and the ultimate need to create a romance.

That Edna Earle Ponder is a respectable Southerner can be seen through those of her comments that illuminate the opinions she holds of the Southern character as a regional phenomenon. The earliest definition, and one that holds throughout the tale, is a definition by contrast.

> I used to dread he might get hold
> of one of these occasional
> travelers that wouldn't come in
> unless they had to -- the kind that
> would break in on a story with a
> set of questions and wind it up
> with a list of what Uncle Daniel's
> faults were: some Yankee.[4]

The passage establishes by contrast what Edna Earle thinks is perhaps the most prized Southern characteristic -- the ability to listen to, and to appreciate, a story. With the passage, Edna Earle not only evokes the tradition of Southern manners, but also insures herself an audience. If the tradition dictates a certain listener's etiquette, then crossing the boundaries of that etiquette defines the listener as a Yankee by association. Listening thus partakes of a correlative characteristic -- Southern hospitality. One accepts what one is offered, whether the gift be a meal or a story. Extended to the family, hospitality involves staying put.[5] As in Delta Wedding, therefore, leaving home is regarded as a variety of death which anyone with breeding and a sense of family duty will avoid.

The gracious acceptance of what is as graciously offered involves a third characteristic, the compounded pride of giver and receiver. Much of Uncle Daniel's pride, for example, revolves around indiscriminate gift-giving (ice cream to a group of chorus girls at the local fair, p. 15), and equally unlooked for gift-receiving (the unquestioned acceptance of Bonnie Dee's surprise return from Memphis, p. 45). Neil D. Isaacs, in Eudora Welty, identifies the pride of the Ponders as a "social pride," and believes it to be the family's central and defining characteristic.[6] Although Edna Earle considers the Ponders the best family in Clay (pp. 6-7), as does Narciss in associating herself with Grandpa Ponder's Studebaker (p.

25), excessive pride is not restricted to the Ponder family alone. Johnnie Ree's performance at Uncle Daniel's trial, for example, focuses the collective pride of the Peacocks on her ability to outwit the lawyer DeYancey Clanahan (p. 94), and the townspeople's pride appears symbolically in the cakes and pies sent to Uncle Daniel as personal remembrances the week of the trial (p. 61).[7]

The primary example of regional myth, however, is the extended description of Uncle Daniel as typical Southern Cavalier.[8] The tableau is a composite outlined by Edna Earle early in the narrative and amplified throughout.

> You'd know it was Uncle
> Daniel the minute you saw him.
> He's unmistakable. He's big and
> well known. He has the Ponder head
> -- large, of course, and well set,
> with short white hair over it
> thick and curly, growing down his
> forehead round like a little bib.
> He has Grandma's complexion. And
> big, forget-me-not blue eyes like
> mine, and puts on a sweet red bow
> tie every morning, and carries a
> large-size Stetson in his hand --
> always just swept it off to some-
> body. He dresses fit to kill, you
> know, in a snow-white suit. (p. 6)

The initial portrait is rounded by the addition of detail in much the same way that a basic recipe is enhanced by adding a pinch of several spices at appropriate times during preparation.[9] Uncle Daniel's white suit and Stetson come to connote a style of grandeur based on gesture ("... Uncle Daniel came in behind her and after he kissed Grandpa, stepped to the mantel and rested his elbow on it in a kind of grand way," p. 28), association with both politics (Edna Earle associated him first with a Senator, p. 30, and later with a candidate, p. 97) and old money (p. 35), and the innate "gift" of knowing how to dress well (pp. 21, 62). It is to this image of Uncle Daniel that Edna Earle is loyal, just as it is around this image that many of the tale's ironies revolve.

Loyalty, like the etiquette of listening, derives from a sense of duty. In their book Invisible Loyal-

ties: Reciprocity in Intergenerational Therapy, Ivan
Boszormenyi-Nagy and Geraldine Spark define the terms
as follows:

> The concept of a multipersonal
> loyalty fabric ... implies the
> existence of structured group
> expectations to which all members
> are committed. In this sense,
> loyalty pertains to what Buber
> called 'the order of the human
> world.' Its frame of reference is
> trust, merit, commitment, and
> action ...[10]

Edna Earle's loyalty is "multipersonal" in that it
refers as much to Grandpa (both in his life and after
his death) as to Uncle Daniel. When she hears DeYancey
tell an anecdote about Grandpa's implication that Uncle
Daniel is brainless, her response is typically one of
loyalty to both Ponders: "Let me go, DeYancey, I
haven't got time for conversation. I have to get out
there and stand up for both of them" (p. 28). Her
loyalty here, as elsewhere, is protective of family
myth (in this case, the myth that Uncle Daniel is not
brainless). In defending both Grandpa and Uncle
Daniel, Edna Earle is defending her own identity and
history as a Ponder. Again to quote Invisible
Loyalties:

> Nations, religious groups, fami-
> lies, professional groups, etc.,
> have their own myths and legends
> to which each member is expected
> to be loyal. National loyalty is
> based on cultural identity, iden-
> tificational, common territory,
> and shared history...[11]

For Edna Earle, Clay can be divided between those who
are and those who are not "friends of the Ponders" (p.
59) -- that is, loyal to their myth. Judge Tip
Clanahan clearly belongs to the former but his participation is ironic. Edna Earle explains the judge as the
man who gets the Ponders "out of fixes" (p. 25), but
her narrative reveals him instead as kindly and
elderly, but ineffectual. His loyalty to the Ponders
is the de facto result of a shared history and,
although Edna Earle asserts that the judge is capable
of disentangling their legal difficulties, the reader
learns that Judge Tip is not in fact a judge (p. 60),

that he spends most of his days asleep in his office
(p. 26), and that he has long ago bequeathed the
Ponders to his grandson, DeYancey, even though he
insists he has not.

The cavalier image of Uncle Daniel that Edna Earle
projects similarly becomes ironic when viewed within
the context of her narrative. Uncle Daniel's soft-
headedness and resulting hospitalization contradict
the image Edna Earle has created of him, and the
disparity is pushed to its ironic limit when Uncle
Daniel's cavalier appearance and manner lead to an
incident of mistaken identity.

> Uncle Daniel was far and away the
> best dressed and most cheerful of
> the two, of course. Uncle Daniel
> says, 'Man alive! Don't you know
> that's Mr. Ponder?' And the lady
> was loading the Coca-Cola machine
> says, 'Oh, foot, I can't remember
> everybody,' and called somebody
> and they took Grandpa. (p. 12)

The mistake the woman makes in the above passage is
believing in the image she sees. Uncle Daniel's soft-
headedness is, in fact, an extended parody of the
casual Southern Planter as defined by Rollin G.
Osterweis in Romanticism and Nationalism in the Old
South.

> The Southern Planter stood at the
> top of a stratified society,
> cherishing the country-gentleman
> ideal -- his lordly sense of
> leadership fed by the presence of
> slaves. His code commanded cour-
> tesy, deference to women, hospi-
> tality to strangers, defense of
> his honor, consideration for
> social inferiors.[12]

Uncle Daniel thus has the heart (that is, the inclina-
tions) of the Southern Planter class without the mind
needed to complete the ideal.

Charles E. Davis has suggested, in "The South in
Eudora Welty's Fiction: A Changing World,"[13] that
Welty's characters can be understood in terms of their
conflict with the changing environments they inhabit.

61

One of the ironies of the mistaken identity episode is, in effect, the disparity between the ante-bellum and twentieth-century Southerner expressed in Uncle Daniel's introduction of Grandpa Ponder and the response it elicits. The clash between cavalier and modern becomes comic when the former's desire to show an elder relative his due respect insures that elder's hospitalization as a mental patient. The irony is enhanced when the reader recalls the unself-conscious revelation of corruption in small-town Southern government with which Edna Earle had begun her anecdote: "Grandpa one time, for a treat, brought Uncle Daniel home to vote ..." (p. 12).

The "displaced" quality of the Ponders is further emphasized in Edna Earle's descriptions of the Beulah Hotel ("It was Grandma's by inheritance, and used to be perfectly beautiful before it lost its paint, and the sign and the trees blew down in front ...", p. 7), and the Ponder place (painted "bright as a railroad station" and sprinkled with lightning rods, p. 31). Like Uncle Daniel, hotel and house are grotesque remnants of a mythologized past. They become ironic through Edna Earle's perception of them not as anti-quated symbols of the ante-bellum period, but rather as part of a continuing romantic fiction grounded solidly in the present. What she sees in each is not the building itself, but rather the significance of "place." Hotel and house are Edna Earle's touchstones in a world revealed through her narrative. They form the center of a landscape that we watch radiate out into Clay and beyond, diminishing in stature and blurring in clarity the farther we look from them.

Edna Earle establishes a value system, in the first few pages of the narrative, based on geographic positioning in relation to herself. Obviously, kin (the inhabitants of house and hotel) form the nucleus of the system. Next in importance are the local towns-people (whom Edna Earle identifies as "responsible"), and the outer ring is composed of "strangers" (a class as suspect as those "up to something," p. 8).[14] The value system provides a grid upon which character can be plotted according to "place." As in <u>Delta Wedding</u>, therefore, <u>who</u> one is can be answered in large part by <u>where</u> one <u>is</u>. For example, much of Uncle Daniel's difficulty throughout the narrative is, as Edna Earle explains to Mr. Springer, the result of "straying too far from where you're known and all -- having too wide a territory" (p. 13). Silver City is regarded as "too progressive" precisely because it is composed of people, like the woman at the asylum, who don't recognize a Ponder when they see one (p. 23). In Clay, however, "everybody knows where everybody is, if they really want to find them" (p. 41), and the ability to plot townspeople on a geographic grid is a source of comfort not only to Edna Earle, but also to Uncle Daniel, as, for example, when Bonnie Dee returns from Memphis and sends him to the Beulah Hotel: "And to tell you the truth, he was happy. This time, he knew where she was" (p. 48)

In "Dialogue as a Reflection of Place in The Ponder Heart," Robert B. Holland sees each character as belonging to two families, one of blood and one of region.[15] Grandpa, Uncle Daniel, and Edna Earle can, however, be said to gain a sense of identity as much from Clay as from one another because in the world of Clay as graphed by Edna Earle's value system, the two categories are nearly synonymous. The way in which character belongs to place, however, is ambivalent. Family and place conspire in Clay, as in Shellmound of Delta Wedding, not only to provide security but also to impose restrictions. When Uncle Daniel wishes to marry Bonnie Dee Peacock, therefore, he must travel to Silver City, a place in which he is unknown, but one in which he is free to do as he pleases. In Clay, Uncle Daniel is known and loved, but hampered; in Silver City (or anywhere else symbolic of a modern, industrial society), he is isolated and alienated, but left in peace. This paradox of a love that imprisons is neatly expressed in a conversation[16] Edna Earle relates early in her narrative.

> I said, 'Dear heart, I know the asylum's no place for you, but neither is the top of a real high mountain or a cave in the cold dark ground. Here's the place.' And he said, 'All right, Edna Earle, but make me some candy.' (p. 10)

The passage suggests the doubleness of a community in which togetherness verges on what Andrew Lytle has termed "the incest of the spirit."[17] It is the community that has imploded, if you will, the community in which news is gossip and history anecdote.

The Southern community as presented in The Ponder Heart can be defined as a thematic "isogloss," or dia-

lect boundary,[18] by the gossip and anecdote inherent to
it. The line marking Edna Earle's territory, or home
turf, is precisely the point at which she must[19] begin
explaining the geographic, or local, legends that
comprise the communal language she understands and is
understood by. In Clay, news travels by word of mouth,
and word of mouth is the medium of gossip. The transmission of news takes several forms in the tale ranging
from the simple to the complex. When trying to fetch
Dr. Ewbanks, Edna Earle hollers to a boy on a hay wagon
("I never thought of the telephone!" p. 106), and
Bonnie Dee similarly relies on messengers to conjure
Uncle Daniel ("She sent it by three different people --
the ice man, the blackberry lady, and the poor blind
man with the brooms that liked to never found me, but
he told it the best." p. 54). Although Edna Earle
attributes the communication of much Ponder news to Eva
Sistrunk, who is neither above listening in on family
business face to face (pp. 22, 51), nor joining in on
the telephone (p. 27), she also assumes that what is
personal is ultimately communal as well (pp. 28, 61).

Just as news has become gossip, so history has
been reduced to the encapsulating anecdote. Hearing
from Judge Tip about Uncle Daniel's extravagance in
treating the chorus girls to ice cream is such a power-
ful statement of character that the very anecdote gives
Grandpa "a spell with his heart" (p. 16). On a broader
level, the narrative itself is the communal history of
Uncle Daniel's relationship to the town of Clay
"created," as Douglas Messerli states in "Metronome and
Music: The Encounter Between History and Myth in The
Golden Apples," "by the historian taking events in
linear time and reinterpreting them according to his
vision of reality."[20] Although anecdote, like gossip,
is public, it shares an etiquette not unlike that of
listening discussed above. Judge Tip can therefore
acquaint Grandpa with information that Edna Earle keeps
to herself, just as the townspeople can be familiar
with Uncle Daniel's marriage to Bonnie Dee, and yet not
want to hear it from Gladney the day of the trial (p.
98).

If love imprisons, then so does news. Uncle
Daniel must travel to Silver City to escape his
regional as well as his blood family because, as we
have said, the two share a geographic isogloss. The
notion of family in The Ponder Heart therefore suggests
a network of individuals sharing a communal language
that in turn defines and sustains them. Because the

narrative itself partakes of this language, it supplies
enough information about members of the regional family
to enable us to plot them according to Edna Earle's
value system. The space of the story is therefore the
mind-space of a town filtered through one of its
participant observers. It is a region in which deeds
are, as Robert B. Holland has noted,[21] subordinate to
words, and one in which language gives shape to
identity and meaning to name.

As in Delta Wedding, family myth is here sustained
and transmitted through speech. On one level, language
is a verbal index of myth encoded in surname. Edna
Earle's comments about individual families within Clay
are a way of plotting those families hierarchically in
relation to the Ponders. The classification refines
the qualitative split between those who are and those
who are not friends of the Ponders to a quantitative
degree. The Bodkins, for example, are dismissed in
Edna Earle's inference that only a stranger would allow
one of them to fix his car (p. 6), and despite Miss
Teacake Magee's name Edna Earle knows that "she's a
Sistrunk" (p. 17), and that "the Sistrunks are all
Baptists -- big Baptists" (p. 14). That the status of
the Sistrunks is close enough to rival that of the
Ponders can be assumed from the verbal mud-slinging
that follows Uncle Daniel's trial.

> 'Well,' says Miss Missionary
> Sistrunk -- the oldest one, re-
> turned from wildest Africa just
> twenty-four hours before -- 'the
> Ponders as I've always been told
> did not burn their cotton when
> Sherman came, and maybe this is
> their judgment.'
>   'Take that back, Miss
> Florette,' I says over people's
> heads. 'The Ponders did not make
> their money that way. You got
> yours suing,' I says. 'What if
> that train hadn't hit Professor
> Magee, where'd any Sistrunks be
> today? Ours was pine trees and
> 'way after Sherman, and you know
> it.' (p. 109)[22]

Both Edna Earle and Miss Missionary Sistrunk aim their
attacks at the level of family myth as sustained and
transmitted over time. The marriage of Uncle Daniel to

a Peacock shortly after the demise of his union with Miss Teacake Magee is similarly a family mortification to both Ponders and Sistrunks (p. 29) because it aligns them with a family incapable of description other than as "plain folk."[23]

> The Peacocks are the kind of people keep the mirror outside on the front porch, and go out and pick railroad lilies to bring inside the house, and wave at trains till the day they died. (p. 20)

Edna Earle's low opinion of the Peacocks is more often reserved for the condemning aside ("just like any Peacock would be bound to do," p. 49; "Bonnie Dee, with her origins," p. 34) with which she similarly reduces Dorris R. Gladney: "Walked too low, and got up and down too fast, like all the Gladneys" (p. 64).

The family that supplies the standard by which all others are judged is obviously the Ponder family. To Edna Earle, the Ponders are "prominent" (pp. 34, 113), popular (p. 62), and honest (p. 79), but flawed by "the Ponder heart" (p. 16) -- " a fond and loving heart" (p. 26) which insures that, as Edna Earle puts it, "we run to sudden ends, all we Ponders" (p. 29). The Ponder heart (most notable in Uncle Daniel) is countered by the Ponder head (most notable in Grandpa), which Edna Earle describes as large (p. 6) and intelligent (p. 24). Together heart and head constitute what Neil D. Isaacs calls "a self-projected legend"[24] composed of intense generosity and extreme intelligence. Edna Earle's sense of superiority (pp. 5, 41) stems from her belief not only in the legend but also in her self-appointed place within it. The designation is ironic in that Edna Earle may well be Grandpa's "favorite grandchild" simply because she is "the only one left alive or in calling distance" (p. 4). Further ironies include the fact that Edna Earle does not see herself as an "old maid" (although her last ability to marry may have vanished with Mr. Springer) as long as she can elicit "a pinch of some kind from a Clanahan" (p. 60), and that she persists in believing in the power of the Ponder name even when the ferris wheel operator refuses to let her off "no matter how often I told them who I was" (p. 15).

Perhaps more than any of her other qualities, however, real or imagined, Edna Earle believes in her ability to "size people up": "I don't run the Beulah Hotel for nothing: I size people up: I'm sizing you up right now" (p. 6). The hotel register thus becomes a metaphor of sorts for the catalogue of names recalled in the narrative and given shape by Edna Earle's opinions of the people they signify. Like classification by surname, "sizing people up" is a means of identification transmitted publicly through gossip or anecdote and based on a personal value system. The way Edna Earle sizes people up is by measuring their behavior or etiquette to her standards as a Ponder. Occasionally she will comment on her own behavior, as, for example, when she counts railroad cars at Bonnie Dee's funeral -- "not because I didn't know any better, like them, but because I couldn't help it right then" (p. 58) -- or when she allows herself a sigh after Uncle Daniel has decided to take the witness stand at his trial -- "I just drew a deep, big sigh. Sometimes I do that, but not like then, in public" (p. 96). More often, however, her censorship is aimed at the behavior of others. Uncle Daniel's refrain "where has Bonnie Dee gone?" (pp. 40, 41), for example, draws both a right

> ... the Clay people cheering him on, clapping him on the shoulder. Everybody here, young or old, knew what to say as well as he did. (p. 37)

and a wrong

> Somebody'd always be fool enough to ask Uncle Daniel how come he didn't hop in his car and drive on up to Memphis and look for Bonnie Dee, if he wanted her back that bad. (pp. 37-8)

response from his listeners, and it is the taking of Uncle Daniel's money rather than his giving of it after the trial that Edna Earle deplores: "You know, I think people have lost the power to be ashamed of themselves" (p. 109). Much of Edna Earle's sense of propriety is revealed through her observations at the trial itself. The Peacocks are the most blatant misbehavers according to Edna Earle, for they are inappropriately dressed and assembled (p. 63), their dinner basket draws ants

throughout Edna Earle's testimony (p. 89), their water-
melon rinds are left "lying on the Courthouse grass for
the world to see and pick up" (p. 90), and their dog
barks "incessantly at all the dogs in town from the
Courthouse porch" (p. 63). Edna Earle, whose self-
portrait suggests proper courtroom demeanor ("I kept my
gloves on, and shook open my Japanese fan, and just
fanned" p. 62), notes that Narciss is no better than
the Peacocks, for she brings her dog to the witness
stand -- "she didn't know any better than to let him
come, so there he trotted" (p. 70).

Bonnie Dee's funeral provides an earlier opportunity for Edna Earle to comment on the behavior of the
Peacocks, this time within a setting provided by the
townspeople of Polk.

> During the service, half the
> Peacocks -- the girls -- were
> still as mice, but the boys, some
> of them grown men, were all
> collected out on the porch. Do you
> know what they did out there, on
> the other side of the wall from us?
> Bawled. Howled. Not that they
> ever did a thing for their sister
> in life, very likely, or even came
> to see her, but now they decided to
> let forth. And do you know all
> through everything the broom was
> still standing behind the door in
> that room? (p. 57)

Mrs. Peacock wears tennis shoes to her daughter's
funeral ("I guess she couldn't help it"), her floor is
full of cracks and sprinkled with chickens, and the
coffin is laid across the hearth, where Bonnie Dee is
exhibited in a "Sunday-go-to-meeting dress, old-timey
looking and too big for her -- never washed or worn,
just saved" (p. 56). The Peacocks gain their identity
as much from Polk as do the Ponders from Clay, and
their inability to behave properly is, in part, a
reflection of "place." The reason that Bonnie Dee has
escaped classification with them to the extent that she
has can be explained by the fact that she has traded
the isogloss of Polk for that of Clay.

> Of course, Polk did use to be on
> the road. But the road left and it
> didn't get up and follow, and

68

```
                  neither  did  the  Peacocks.   Up un-
                  til Bonnie Dee. (p. 58)
```

Edna Earle's explanation reveals both her ethnocentricity and the degree to which behavior and identity partake of "place."

    The combination of gossip, anecdote, and family myth result in the concept of "story." Telling one's own or someone else's story is a way of revealing that person's character or signature. Once it has taken place, story becomes public property. When visitors arrive at the Beulah Hotel, therefore, the best way that Uncle Daniel can give them a tour of Clay is through story.

```
                  He  took  every  soul  I  let  in  at  the
                  Beulah   straight   to   his   heart.
                  'Hello,  son -- what's  news?'  --
                  then  he'd  start  in.    Oh,  the
                  stories!  He made free with every-
                  body's  --  he'd  tell  yours  and  his
                  and  the  Man  in  the  Moon's.   (p.
                  51)
```

Miss Teacake Magee, Elsie Flemming, Dorris R. Gladney, Bonnie Dee Peacock and her sister Johnnie Ree, Eva Sistrunk -- all have their stories in The Ponder Heart. Edna Earle transmits Miss Teacake's story to her listener in one sentence: "Miss Teacake Magee is of course a Sistrunk (the Sistrunks are all Baptists --big Baptists) and Professor Magee's widow" (p. 14). In defining Miss Teacake for the listener, Edna Earle has told her story: born a Sistrunk, married to Professor Magee, widowed. None of the details Edna Earle gives about her reflect the identity of Miss Teacake in terms other than those of the community of Clay. Edna Earle's language itself indicates a habit of equating identity with story, and it is this equation that enables her to dismiss Miss Teacake in the phrase "so Miss Teacake's an old story" (p. 23) when Uncle Daniel drives into Clay with Bonnie Dee Peacock.

    Characters, like Intrepid Elsie Flemming and Dorris R. Gladney, who appear only tangentially in the narrative, are similarly shaped by story. Edna Earle's sketch of the former, for example, first establishes her communal identity as the motorcycle-performer who rides around the Wall of Death at the Clay Fair, and then isolates her story in the detail "she dressed up

in pants" (p. 15). The conjunction of the two details
reveals all we need to know about Intrepid Elsie: she
is a masculine woman. Dorris R. Gladney is similarly
identified first by community -- "that country attorney
we wished on ourselves" (p. 59) -- and then by descrip-
tive detail -- "long, black, buzzardly coat, black
suspenders, beaky nose, and on his little finger a
diamond bigger than mine, but not half as expensive"
(p. 64). In the event that the significance of the
last detail has eluded her audience, Edna Earle trans-
lates Gladney's story several pages later: "Grandma
Ponder said, 'Show me a man wears a diamond ring and
I'll show you a wife beater.' There he was" (p. 96).

The stories of Bonnie Dee Peacock and Eva Sistrunk
are slightly more complex. Edna Earle initially
describes Bonnie Dee as "a little thing with yellow,
fluffy hair" (p. 20), "seventeen years old and seemed
like she just stayed seventeen", who knows how to make
change and cut hair (p. 30). A few pages later,
however, Edna Earle attempts to understand Bonnie Dee
through her relationship to community or "place."

> The way I look at Bonnie Dee,
> her story was this. She'd come up
> from the country -- and before she
> knew it, she was right back in the
> country. Married or no. She was
> away out yonder on Ponder Hill and
> nothing to do and nothing to play
> with in sight but the Negroes'
> dogs and the Peppers' cats and one
> little frizzly hen. From the kind
> of long pink fingernails she kept
> in the ten cent store, that hadn't
> been her idea at all. Not her
> dream. (p. 34)

Unlike Miss Teacake Magee, Intrepid Elsie Flemming, and
Dorris R. Gladney, Bonnie Dee had wanted something from
"place." Her story can therefore be seen as a parody
of the Southern Belle in the twentieth century -- a
seventeen-year-old-girl ordering new clothes and gad-
gets from catalogs (p. 49). Johnnie Ree, the echo of
her sister ("the same size and the same hair," p. 90)
in name, clothes, and style, both completes the parody
of the Southern Belle and creates her own story through
her performance at Uncle Daniel's trial. In outwitting
DeYancey Clanahan, Johnnie Ree accomplishes the
linguistic equivalent in Polk of being "valedictorian

70

of the graduating class" (p. 94). It is the sham attainment of a status Bonnie Dee was trying to escape -- e.g., being "country."

The notion of being "country" can best be seen in Eva Sistrunk who, unlike Bonnie Dee Peacock, is comfortable with "place." If, as we have previously noted, Edna Earle attributes the transmission of much Ponder business in Clay to Eva, then she also uses Eva as an index of community feeling. When Uncle Daniel visits the Beulah Hotel night after night only to retell the news of Bonnie Dee's departure, for example, it is Eva who voices the feeling that the habit may or may not be good for the Hotel (pp. 36-7). During her testimony at Uncle Daniel's trial, Edna Earle is reassured that community sentiment may be on her side when she sees Eva take out her handkerchief and weep (p. 85). And, after Uncle Daniel has been acquitted and has alienated himself from the community by giving away all his money in court, Edna Earle measures the duration of their isolation by Eva's absence: "You'd think Eva Sistrunk, at least, would be beginning to get lonesome" (p. 116). Given her function as the index of community feeling, therefore, it is not insignificant that Eva's signature, or talent, is drawing the coat-of-arms of every family in Clay (p. 53).

The concept of the story is crucial to <u>The Ponder Heart</u> because it necessitates the acceptance of the story-teller as narrative authority. If we follow Neil D. Isaacs' definition of the narrative as a "performance story,"[25] then we must accept <u>The Ponder Heart</u> within the tradition of oral narrative. In <u>The Nature of Narrative</u>, Robert Scholes and Robert Kellogg argue that "the oral tradition is both the story and the author,"[26] so that in order to believe in the former, we must also believe in the latter. Edna Earle insures her credibility through two devices: reference to the townspeople for collaboration or witnessing, and reference to the listener for verification. When describing Uncle Daniel's marriage jaunt to Silver City, for example, Edna Earle stresses the fact that none of the townspeople stopped them from going because none of the townspeople saw them leave.

> ... Narciss hitched herself right in that front seat and up to the wheel and here they flew; got Bonnie Dee from in front of Woolworth's (and nobody saw it, which

71

> I think is worth mentioning) and
> went kiting off to Silver City
> .... (p. 23)

Bonnie Dee's disappearance, on the other hand, is witnessed by several townspeople who watch her flag the
north-bound bus.

> A dozen people must have been in
> the bushes and seen her, or known
> somebody that did, and they all
> came and told me about it. (p. 33)

The story of Bonnie Dee's disappearance is thus as con-
cretely known as is "the little blue-fig tree the
Ponders have always had in their yard, known to all"
(p. 74) that DeYancey enters as evidence in Uncle
Daniel's trial. And even Edna Earle is forced to
accept the possibility that "there are worthwhile
Peacocks" when "Miss Lutie Powell has vouched for it to
Eva Sistrunk" (p. 58).

Edna Earle relies on her listener for verification
throughout the narrative, and verification takes the
form of questioning. Edna Earle's questions become
more meaningful the longer she talks. Her first questions ("... see what a large head size he wears?" p.
3; "... do you know he's up in his fifties now?" p. 6)
pertain to Uncle Daniel's physical appearance and are
primarily rhetorical. Later in the narrative, however,
she establishes Uncle Daniel's intelligence ("He's
smart in a way you aren't, child" p. 51) and begins to
align the listener's point of view with her own: "...
he didn't mind old dirty people the way you and I do"
(p. 67). The listener is brought into both town and
family through hearing about them from Edna Earle. The
more she tells, therefore, the stronger she feels the
bond between the subject of her narration and its
hearer. This process is illustrated first in Edna
Earle's mention of the "premonition" she feels the day
of Bonnie Dee's death (p. 54), and later in the
reference not back to her story but back to the premonition itself: "... but I went right on and said I
had a premonition. You remember it" (p. 83). What the
listener remembers, of course, is where the premonition
occurred in the story rather than the actual feeling
Edna Earle experienced. The identification Edna Earle
makes is between subject and hearer, and is completed
in her final questions to the listener: "Could I go on
letting Uncle Daniel think that was the right way to be

happy? Could you let your uncle?" (p. 50); "You don't
think I betrayed him by not letting him betray himself,
do you?" (p. 110). That Edna Earle can ask questions
as profound as these of someone learning Uncle Daniel's
story at several removes is a testament to the
listener's acceptance of her as narrative authority.

When Edna Earle describes herself as "the go-
between, that's what I am, between my family and the
world" (p. 89), she is making a statement about art.
If the performance story is an art form, then Edna
Earle is, quite literally, the medium through which
family myth is translated to the world. In a sense,
the label of "go-between" is ironic in that Edna Earle
obstructs the direct relationship between listener and
myth as much as she creates it. That is, Edna Earle
illuminates Uncle Daniel's story, but only according to
her own lights. The myth she narrates becomes ironic,
therefore, when viewed through the "conceptual blocks"
that form her mental space.²⁷ Several ironies surface
in the narrative, and serve to accentuate the distance
between the mental space of Clay and that of Edna
Earle's listener and/or reader. Among them are her
insistence, midway through her uninterrupted narrative, that "I hardly ever get a word in for myself" (p.
89), and DeYancey's refusal to call Uncle Daniel, who
loves talk as much as he loves the limelight, to the
witness stand. Similar ironies reside in the testimony
of Mr. Truex Bodkin, the blind coroner (p. 64), and
Judge Waite's interruption of Miss Teacake's testimony
to count a show of hands for those intending to eat
noon dinner at the Beulah (pp. 68-9).

The narrative's primary ironies, however, are
found in the repetition of incident. As in The Robber
Bridegroom and Delta Wedding, time in The Ponder Heart
is measured by event. Thus, the habit Grandpa and
Uncle Daniel have of going to town each Saturday comes
to signify both time and place to the townspeople of
Clay:

> That was the way you knew where you
> were and the day of the week it was
> -- those two hats announcing them-
> selves, rounding the square and
> making it through the crowd. (p.
> 7)

And in Miss Teacake Magee's life, time and event revert
to only one formulation: "Since I lost Professor

73

Magee" (p. 14). The most significant event in the Ponder family, however, and one that accounts for the narrative's central irony, is the murder of Bonnie Dee Peacock. Over half of the narrative revolves around versions of the murder (pp. 60-102) supplied by Mr. Truex Bodkin, Big John, Miss Teacake Magee, Narciss, Dr. Ewbanks, Edna Earle, and Uncle Daniel. In these pages, the content of the narrative (repetition of, or circling around, event) mimics narrative form (Edna Earle's delight at receiving company for Uncle Daniel's sake, which begins and ends the story). The events of the murder itself (Bonnie Dee laughs to death while Uncle Daniel tickles her between the shoulders, playing "creep-mousie" with Grandma's antimacassar tassle, p. 103) are never revealed in court because, as Edna Earle knows, "nobody'll believe it" (p. 106). In a sense, therefore, the event of Bonnie Dee's death does not correspond to the truth of the way she died. The irony inherent to the event is that Bonnie Dee was murdered by Uncle Daniel's love of her.[28] According to Ruth M. Vande Kieft, the irony can be seen as tragic because, like many of Welty's ironies, it is "the result of an external catastrophe which brings the individual up against the enigma of the universe."[29] The distinction is reminiscent of Northrop Frye's differentiation between historian (whose concern is with what happened) and poet (whose concern is with what happens),[30] in that both point toward a disjunction between individual event and universal truth. In her review of William Faulkner's Intruder in the Dust, Welty comments on the power of the story to reveal truth:

> Put one of his stories into a sin-
> gle factual statement and it's
> pure outrage -- so would life be --
> too terrifying, too probable and
> too symbolic too, too funny to
> bear. There has to be the story to
> bear it.[31]

As Edna Earle puts it, "maybe what's hard to believe about the truth is who it happens to" (p. 106).

The belief in language to order chaos is a way of coming to terms with event. There is an element of needing to tell her version of Uncle Daniel's story that is not unlike Uncle Daniel's need to repeat his version of Bonnie Dee's (p. 36), and we are made to feel that Edna Earle, like Uncle Daniel, "never was a bit of good with nothing to talk about" (p. 48). It

74

is, in fact, having to tell a story (no matter whose) that makes company better than love.

> There's something I think's better
> to have than love, and if you want
> me to, I'll tell you what it is --
> that's company. (p. 40)

If giving is sublimated love, then love is sublimated company. Uncle Daniel's proposal to Bonnie Dee, for example, is the inevitable product of the conjunction of Uncle Daniel, audience, and love-object.

> He was intending to tell his story
> in there, I think, but instead of
> that, he was saying to the world in
> general and Bonnie Dee at the
> jewelry counter in particular,
> 'I've got a great big house stand-
> ing empty, and my father's Stude-
> baker. Come on -- marry me.' (p.
> 21)

Uncle Daniel's giving "comes in sprees" (p. 5) that are relieved by "having so much to tell" (p. 11) -- that is, by having company to talk to. For Uncle Daniel, therefore, love and giving are transmitted through language, which in turn informs and gives meaning to both. As Edna Earle realizes when speaking of the violence of the Ponder language,

> It's all in a way of speaking ...
> Putting it into words. With some
> people it's little threats. With
> others, it's liable to be poems.
> (p. 87)

Language is shaped by listener as well as speaker, and it is this linguistic bond that enables Edna Earle to predict Uncle Daniel's message to Bonnie Dee without ever hearing it.

> Mr. Gladney didn't need to traipse
> over the fields and find him an old
> Negro that can't talk good through
> his windpipe to tell the Court
> what word Uncle Daniel sent his
> wife -- I could have repeated it
> without ever hearing it at all, if
> I'd been asked. (p. 82)

Edna Earle can predict Uncle Daniel's words because
language is, in a sense, recipe.

Recipes are a way in which language orders chaos.
One way of defining Polk, for example, is through the
recipe of how to get there.

> You start out like you were going
> to Monterrey, turn at the consol-
> idated school, and bear right till
> you see a Baptist steeple across a
> field, and you just leave the
> gravel and head for that, if you
> have good tires. And that's Polk.
> (p. 55)

Reading directions is, in this case, a way of orienting
oneself in relation to the world. Directions are for-
mulaic in that they tell the reader how to accomplish a
task, whether it be one of organizing space (driving to
Polk) or organizing time (baking a cake). It is not
surprising, therefore, that Edna Earle, whose narrative is a recipe that orders the chaos inherent to
event, appreciates the significance of a good set of
directions.

> How to put on furniture polish,
> transfer patterns with a hot iron,
> take off corns, I don't care what
> it is. I don't have to do it.
> Sometimes I'd rather sit still a
> minute and read a good quiet set of
> directions through than any story
> you'd try to wish off on me. (p.
> 53)

For Edna Earle, this potential to impose an order on
chaos by following a recipe is what is important not
just in cooking, but in making of cooking a performance. The "fourteen perfect quarts of peach
preserves" (p. 44) that Narciss makes with Edna Earle's
supervision and help are thus a performance in much the
same way that the narrative is a performance story. In
"The Reading and Writing of Short Stories," Welty makes
the connection explicit through the notion that both
preserves and stories communicate: "I think we write
stories in the ultimate hope of communication, but so
do we make jelly in that hope."[32] What is communicated
by each is a formula for ordering chaos. Edna Earle's
tableau of Bonnie Dee "curled up on Grandma's rosewood

sofa" and cutting coupons out of magazines becomes a metaphorical judgment on her ability to order her life with the addition of the last detail, "eating the kind of fudge anybody can make" (p. 46). The degree of Narciss's unhappiness in living at the Beulah is similarly communicated through the deterioration of her cooking ability: "I hate to tell you -- her rice won't stand apart" (p.116).

Belief in the ability of language to order chaos takes other forms as well. There is a fairy tale quality in the way Edna Earle "locks" the Beulah ("... I spoke to it and said 'Burglars, stay away' -- and went out to Ponder Hill in my trusty Ford ..." p. 38), and her poem "Come Back to Clay" not only produces Bonnie Dee Peacock, but also evokes Dorris R. Gladney and a lawsuit (p. 114). Edna Earle's name is itself evocative, and recalls the sentimental and pious heroine of Augusta Evans Wilson's St. Elmo (1867), known for her erudition and virtue.[33] Echoing Wilson's novel is a way of compounding Edna Earle's significance in The Ponder Heart by placing her within a literary tradition that begins to shape the way in which she is perceived as soon as her name is understood. Echoes of the fairy tale and sentimental romance amplify the frame of Edna Earle's narrative by pointing outside it toward larger ways of ordering chaos supplied by the literary traditions they represent.

In a sense, The Ponder Heart is Edna Earle's attempt, to borrow Faulkner's formulation, "to say it all in one sentence, between one Cap and one period."[34] The narrative is, in fact, a composite family portrait taken over time, but one stylized, or edited, by its author. The narrative is therefore paradoxical in that Edna Earle is, to paraphrase Emily Dickinson, telling all the truth but telling it slant.[35] The tension of the narrative thus results from Edna Earle's compulsion to talk on one level, and the irony of what her talk reveals to the listener on another. It is the paradox that Oedipus faced in realizing that knowing oneself may destroy the self. Unlike Oedipus, however, Edna Earle is not cognizant of the paradox her narrative illuminates. Her listener is. What makes the narrative an ironic myth, or romance parody, is, as we have said, the distance between what Edna Earle says and what the reader hears. The narrative is romance translated into parody by the listener. The mythmaking or romanticizing process is therefore what keeps Edna Earle from insight because the need to create a romance

77

is self-protective and insight, for Oedipus, involves suffering. Creating a romance is a way, as Mircea Eliade has noted, to "tolerate history"[36] and endure event. In protecting herself from the isolation and alienation that are the by-products of Uncle Daniel's trial, Edna Earle is defending the romance most important to her because, quite literally, the closest to home -- i.e., that of Uncle Daniel and the Ponder heart.

NOTES

[1] Robert B. Holland, "Dialogue as a Reflection of Place in The Ponder Heart." American Literature, 35 (November 1963), pp. 354-7. Holland defines the elements as: a three-stress structure, highly-metered speech, rhythm in structure and substance (e.g., platitude), gossip, euphemism, and exaggeration.

[2] Ruth M. Vande Kieft, in Eudora Welty (New York: Twayne Publishers, Inc., 1962), quotes Welty as saying that "except for what's personal, there is really so little to tell, and that little lacking in excitement and drama in the way of the world" (p. 15).

[3] Northrop Frye, "New Directions from Old," Myth and Mythmaking, Ed. Henry A. Murray. New York: George Braziller, Inc., 1960, p. 117.

[4] Eudora Welty, The Ponder Heart (New York: Harcourt, Brace & World, Inc., 1954), p. 11. Subsequent references to this text will be included parenthetically after the quotation.

[5] On page 39, for example, Edna Earle explains her reasons for being in Clay: "But all the other children and grandchildren went away to the ends of the earth or died and left only me and Uncle Daniel -- the two favorites. So we couldn't leave each other."

[6] Neil D. Isaacs, Eudora Welty (Austin, Texas: Steck-Vaughn Co., 1969), p. 12.

[7] In "The Flavor of Jackson" (The Eye of the Story. New York: Random House, Inc., 1978), Eudora Welty equates the invention or modification of recipe with the individual responsible for it, so that "however often the recipes were made after that by others, they kept their right names" (p. 324).

[8] In Cavalier & Yankee: The Old South and American National Character (New York: Harper & Row, Inc., 1957), William R. Taylor traces the origin of the term to the royal party, or English Cavaliers, thought to have settled the South in Colonial times (p. 15).

[9]The figure of speech is not accidental, and I will be treating the narrative as recipe later in this study.

[10]_Invisible Loyalties: Reciprocity in Intergenerational Therapy_. Eds. Ivan Boszormenyi-Nagy and Geraldine Spark (New York: Medical Dept., Harper & Row, 1973), p. 37.

[11]Ibid., p. 40.

[12]Rollin G. Osterweis, _Romanticism and Nationalism in the Old South_ (New Haven: Yale University Press, 1949), p. 17.

[13]Charles E. Davis, "The South in Eudora Welty's Fiction: A Changing World." _Studies in American Fiction_, 3 (Autumn, 1975), pp. 199-209.

[14]Edna Earle's criticism of Judge Waite much later in the narrative is along these lines: "And Judge Waite wasn't even born in this county" (p. 108).

[15]Robert B. Holland, "Dialogue as a Reflection of Place in _The Ponder Heart_," p. 353.

[16]For an extended discussion of paradox in _The Ponder Heart_ see Robert Y. Drake, Jr., "The Reasons of the Heart." _Georgia Review_, 11 (Winter 1957), pp. 420-426.

[17]Andrew Lytle, "The Working Novelist and The Mythmaking Process." _Myth and Mythmaking_. Ed. Henry A. Murray, p. 147.

[18]The term is supplied by Jan Harold Brunvand, in _The Study of American Folklore: An Introduction_ (New York: W.W. Norton & Co., Inc., 1968), p. 40.

[19]Jan Harold Brunvand defines local legends as those "which are closely associated with specific places, either with their names, their geographic features, or their histories," _The Study of American Folklore: An Introduction_, p. 116.

[20]Douglas Messerli, "Metronome and Music: The Encounter Between History and Myth in _The Golden Apples_." _A Still Moment: Essays on the Art of Eudora_

Welty. Ed. John A. Desmond (London: Scarecrow Press, Inc., 1978). p. 83.

[21]Robert B. Holland, "Dialogue as a Reflection of Place in The Ponder Heart," p. 357.

[22]It is ironic in view of this controversy that after Grandpa Ponder's death Mr. Bank Sistrunk is the man responsible for giving Uncle Daniel his three-dollar-a-month allowance.

[23]Frank L. Owsley, Plain Folk of the Old South (Chicago: Quadrangle Books, 1949), pp. 7-8.

[24]Neil D. Isaacs, Eudora Welty, p. 13.

[25]Ibid., p. 5.

[26]Robert Scholes and Robert Kellogg, The Nature of Narrative (London: Oxford University Press, 1966), p. 55.

[27]In Conceptual Blockbusting (San Francisco: San Francisco Book Company, 1976), James L. Adams defines conceptual blocks as the "mental walls which block the problem-solver from correctly perceiving a problem or conceiving its solution" (p. 11).

[28]This formulation is not new. See, for example, Neil D. Isaacs, Eudora Welty, p. 14.

[29]Ruth M. Vande Kieft, Eudora Welty, p. 173.

[30]Northrop Frye, "New Directions from Old." Myth and Mythmaking, p. 116.

[31]Eudora Welty, review of Intruder in the Dust by William Faulkner. The Eye of the Story (New York: Random House, Inc., 1978), p. 209.

[32]Eudora Welty, "The Reading and Writing of Short Stories." Atlantic, 183 (February 1949), p. 54.

[33]Warren French, "A Note on Eudora Welty's The Ponder Heart." College English, 15 (May 1954), p. 474.

[34]Malcolm Cowley, The Faulkner-Cowley File (New York: Viking Press, Inc., 1966), p. 14.

[35]From Poem #1129. The line reads: "Tell all the truth but tell it slant."

[36]Myths, Rites, Symbols: A Mircea Eliade Reader. Ed. Wendell C. Beane, William G. Doty. Vol. 1. (New York: Harper & Row, 1976), p. 103.

CHAPTER IV. - <u>LOSING BATTLES</u>

It was fifteen years before the concerns of <u>The
Ponder Heart</u> and those narratives antedating it came
full circle in the longest of Welty's stories -- <u>Losing
Battles</u>. As many critics have noted,[1] the circle is
itself the novel's primary symbol and lies at the heart
of the classical mythology within which the novel is
set. For like <u>The Robber Bridegroom</u>, <u>Losing Battles</u>
functions as a Southern Romance[2] on both thematic and
stylistic levels. And like <u>The Ponder Heart</u>, it is an
oral narrative, or "performance story"[3] -- that is, a
story told to an audience. Its plot forms, among other
patterns, the circular shape of a journey similar to
that traced in[4] <u>The Odyssey</u>. The first section of
<u>Losing Battles</u>, for example, contains not only the
completion of one journey cycle (Jack's return to
Banner, p. 70), but also the beginning of another
(Jack's quest to return Mrs. Moody's Buick to the ditch
from which he had unknowingly rescued it, p. 103). The
hero's arrival despite great odds (Jack appears the day
before his scheduled release from Parchman), and the
heroine's unwavering fidelity to her husband (Gloria's
patient waiting, p. 19) suggest Homeric parallels[5] that
are amplified in the formal similarities of the two
works. The treatment of Welty's narrative, like[6] that
of Homer's, is primarily cosmic and epic in form, and
it is this form that allows for the completion of the
journey cycle with which each work ends.

Identifying <u>Losing Battles</u> with Homer's <u>Odyssey</u>,
however, does not preclude a like identification with
the Greek tragedians, and here, as elsewhere, Welty
manages to combine without blurring these antithetical
forms. Like Greek tragic drama, therefore, <u>Losing
Battles</u> concerns itself with "human values, with man's
dignity and his individual responsibility, with pro-
blems raised by the existence of evil, by conflicts of
duty and endurance under stress."[7] Thus, if there is a
comic-epic return (e.g., the framework of the reunion)
signalled by arrivals (of family),[8] then there are also
levels of departure ranging from the literal (the
departures of family members for homes in distant coun-
ties), to the metaphorical and sobering, if not tragic
(Grandpa Vaughn's, and more recently, Miss Julia
Mortimer's deaths).[9] The reunion is the circle that
joins these comic and tragic modes, and it is not
insignificant that Granny Vaughn's ninetieth birthday

83

celebration ends with a joining of hands to sing "Blest Be the Tie" (pp. 348-9).

On a mythic level, the reunion is the "go-round," as Aunt Birdie puts it (p. 343) that marks sacred time. In Mircea Eliade's terms,

> ... religious man lives in two kinds of time, of which the more important, sacred time, appears under the paradoxical aspect of a circular time, reversible and recoverable, a sort of eternal mythical present that is periodically reintegrated by means of rites. This attitude in regard to time suffices to distinguish religious from non-religious man; the former refuses to live solely in what, in modern terms, is called the historical present; he attempts to regain a sacred time that, from one point of view, can be homologized into eternity.[10]

Thus, hymn and circle constitute the rite by which the eternal mythical present is reintegrated on a yearly basis.[11] The centripetal force of the rite in keeping the Beecham-Vaughn-Renfro family a cohesive unit is everywhere reinforced in the novel through Welty's symbolic use of circle and cycle concepts both in dialogue and in description. Throughout the reunion, family members congregate in circular patterns, whether en masse to hear the story of how Jack "robbed" Curly Stovall (pp. 76-7), or in the masculine "circles of squatters" (p. 19) that gather in the yard, and individuals such as Jack (who "circle(s) the table at a hop, counting his mother's cakes out loud," p. 74) and Etoyle ("turning herself in circles to make herself dizzy," p. 85) weave private circles of their own.

As in The Robber Bridegroom, however, the circle is subordinate as a myth symbol to its center, what Mircea Eliade has called "the zone of absolute reality."[12] The sexual ritual reenacted by Jack and Gloria takes place within such a circle,

> Around a circle of needles, slick and hot and sweet as skin under them, and dead quiet, they

84

chased each other on the hobble,
fast as children on their knees,
around and around the tree.   (p.
99)

and Granny Vaughn is appropriately encircled by a ring
of her grandsons who confirm her significance through
sight and touch: "They bent above her, squatted before
her, patted her knee, took her by the hand, tried to
kiss her" (p. 351). Gloria is similarly honored prior
to Jack's return by "small girl cousins" who "had been
drawn to her now, and marched in a circle around her"
(p. 29) in a celebration of femininity, a preface to
the circle that later encloses Jack, Gloria, and Lady
May for their reunion within the reunion (p. 90).

On a broader level, the Renfro farm is the traditional location consecrated by Vaughn-Beecham-Renfro
kin as the center of their family circle. When Aunt
Cleo asks where the family gathers from, therefore, the
response to her question indicates that the journey to
Banner is a pilgrimage inward from points on a circle
to its center.

'Everywhere.   Everywhere you
ever heard of in Boone County -- I
can see faces from Banner, Peer-
less,   Wisdom,   Upright,   Morning
Star, Harmony, and Deepstep with
no trouble at all.'
'And this is Banner.   The
very heart,' said Miss Beulah,
calling from the kitchen. (p. 18)

That the Renfro farm is "center stage for the ritual
action that follows" is established by the map, and the
lists of character, time and place with which the novel
is prefaced. The opening pages of the narrative are,
indeed, reminiscent of stage directions that have been
couched within the language of the German märchen. [13]

When the rooster crowed, the
moon had still not left the world
but was going down on flushed
cheek, one day short of the full.
A long thin cloud crossed it
slowly, drawing itself out like a
name being called.   The air
changed, as if a mile or so away a
wooden door had swung open, and a

85

> smell, more of warmth than wet,
> from a river at low stage, moved
> upward into the clay hills that
> stood in darkness.
>   Then a house appeared on its
> ridge, like an old man's silver
> watch pulled once more out of its
> pocket. A dog leaped up from where
> he'd lain like a stone and began
> barking for today as if he meant
> never to stop.
>   Then a baby bolted naked out
> of the house. (p. 3)

Like The Robber Bridegroom, Losing Battles opens upon a
world of enchantment.[14] Here, however, the scene is
evoked by a sunrise that functions in much the same way
as house lights raised upon a set. Character and scene
are more revealed than created, and the overall effect
of these opening pages (if we consider both description
and Welty's "and then" narrative style, to borrow a
term from Northrop Frye)[15] is one of a stage set for
romantic quest. The dreamlike quality,[16] or "benef-
icent aura",[17] noted by some critics in these pages is
merely an evocation of the enchanted world of the
Renfro farm, the unified and harmonious center of the
circle.

    As in The Robber Bridegroom and Delta Wedding,
however, circles can indicate isolation as well as
unity, confusion as well as harmony. Granny Vaughn's
point of view from the center of the circle is, for
example, much different from that of Aunt Cleo, the
outsider to whom the family appears large and frag-
mented (" 'Where they all get here from' cried Aunt
Cleo, looking full circle around her", p. 18), and the
encircling of Granny Vaughn's daughter Ellen is
perceived by Granny as the impersonal circling of
vultures around a carcass ("With Ellen in her coffin,
they came circling round and stripped the ring from her
finger," p. 219). Miss Beulah's recollection of Rachel
Sojourner's taunting ("Yes, in this house, I'd hear the
boys tease her, circling around her ...", p. 253) not
only echoes Gloria's previous encircling by girl
cousins, but also suggests the rite by which she is
later initiated into the family:

> As though in some evening accord
> with the birds, the aunts came
> circling in to Gloria, crowding

86

> Miss Beulah to one side -- all the
> aunts and some of the girl cous-
> ins. (p. 268)

Gloria's encircling, like Granny's recollection of
Ellen's, is ominously linked to the natural world
through identification with the circlings of birds.
Elsewhere in the novel, the futile circlings of Aycock
Comfort's dogs (pp. 131, 392) and the Renfro mule Bet
(p. 207) counterpoint the more inexorable circles that
nature imposes on the reunion. The peephole out of
which Lady May jumps, for example, is a "circle of sky"
(p. 160) that both invites and nearly harms her, and
despite the reunion's wish to stop time, shade circles
from the back to the front yard and morning wheels to
afternoon (p. 175).

The mysterious yet inevitable circles traced in
the natural world are perhaps best understood by the
seemingly erratic cycle of the century plant. Despite
the name, the plant moves on a timeline established and
maintained solely by its species. Its progress toward
blooming is as suspect as it is aweful to the reunion,
to which it is an emblem both of tenacity and of
unintelligibility.

> Little groups in turn looked down
> in a ring at the spectacle, the
> deep white flower, a star inside a
> star, that almost seemed to return
> their gaze, like a member of the
> reunion who didn't invariably come
> when called. (p. 349)

Out of phase with the cycle of day and night, the century plant blooms spectacularly in the stillness and
darkness that follows the reunion, and is only fully
witnessed by Vaughn Renfro, terrified by the exposed
opulence of its flowers.

> Then he saw -- the smell must be
> coming from the flowers. They
> looked like big clods of the moon-
> light freshly turned up from this
> night -- almost phosphorescent.
> All of him shied, as if a harness
> had bloomed. (p. 366)

Once it has bloomed, the century plant begins its cycle
again with the death of its flowers, which "look like

wrung chickens' necks in the morning" (pp. 356, 376).
The plant, like the movement of the sun or the peephole
on Banner Top, exists apart from the human life that
surrounds it (" 'Can't tell a century plant what to
do,' " p. 18), and forms the metaphorical context
within which sacred time acquires meaning.

The reunion itself has a mythic cycle, and one
that, like the cycle of the century plant, operates on
an independent time line. But the relationship of the
reunion to time is paradoxical. As a rite, the reunion
partakes, as we have said, of the eternal mythical present. The roles within that rite, however, are filled
by different family members over time (Brother Bethune,
for example, is "taking Grandpa's place at the reunion"
for Granny Vaughn's ninetieth birthday, p. 103). In
this latter sense, therefore, the mythic configuration
of the rite is only sustained by the replacement of its
various members, so that the reunion (the eternal
mythical present) is dependent upon the very processes
of time that it in turn obliterates. In other words,
in Losing Battles, historical myth (regional, geographic, and family myth) perpetuates classical myth.
If, as Michael Kreyling has asserted,

> ... in Losing Battles myth and
> history battle for the allegiance
> of men's minds and existence, the
> timeless fights the temporal, the
> circle[18] struggles against the
> line,

then the line[19] also creates the circle, which is, in
turn, linear.

The broadest historical myth is the regional myth
of the land. Like the century plant, the land has its
own mysterious cycle. Unlike that of the plant, however, the land's cycle is disturbed by those whose
lives it determines, and is thereby brought into
historical, or linear, time. The fate of those who
depend upon the land is not only determined by the
land's performance, but also by the myth of that performance as extended over time. If, for example, the
Depression years are more difficult for the Vaughn-
Beecham-Renfro family than previous years, it is, as
Uncle Dolphus puts it, " 'the fault of the land going
back on us, treating us the wrong way' " (p. 194). The
land is at fault because it is linked to the farmer
through the concept of "home." In his article "Cir-

cling-In: The Concept of Home in Eudora Welty's <u>Losing Battles</u> and <u>The Optimist's Daughter</u>," William McMillen defines "home" as "the man-made extension of the land."[20] It is in taking on the emotional charge of "home" that the economic relationship between farmer and land becomes an emotional locus, or moral value center. In his excellent study "The Chosen People," Lewis P. Simpson describes this link between economic survival and domestic virtue as the "mystique of the pastoral community."[21] In the terms of regional myth, the land is responsible for both the economic and moral survival of its inhabitants. It is natural, therefore, that Brother Bethune's recital of family history include not only a synopsis of the land's performance up to the Depression years and a projection of better days to come, but also a glorification of the regional myth.

'I don't reckon good old Mississippi's ever been any poorer than she is right now , 'cept when we lost. And in all our glorious state I can't think of any county likelier to take the cake for being the poorest and generally the hardest-suffering than dear old Boone.' Sighs of leisure and praise rose to encourage him, ... (p. 191)

As they cheered him on he called over them, 'We got hay made and in the barn, we'll soon have some fresh meat, the good ladies has stocked the closet shelf with what garden we saved by hauling water. We got milk and butter and eggs, and maybe even after today's slaughter there'll be a few chickens left.' (p. 192)

'Cleo, the old place here was plum stocked with squirrel when we was boys. It was overrun with quail. And if you never saw the deer running in here, I saw 'em. It was filled -- it was filled! -- with every kind of good thing, this old dwelling, ... (p. 193)

89

Even though Mississippi has been economically unstable since the Civil War, regional mythology dictates the existence of an independent South rich in land that has always provided for its people. The arrival of the hoped-for rain only emphasizes the disparity between regional myth and fact, for it falls in the night the century plant blooms (pp. 367-8), just long and hard enough to ruin the hay (p. 373).

A subordinate regional myth, the myth of Southern politics and the Southern politician, operates through a similar ironic disparity. Here, however, the irony revolves around the notion of "kin." Throughout the time frame of the novel, Curly Stoval and Homer Champion are competing for last-minute votes prior to Tuesday's election. The former, who is Jack Renfro's antagonist and the man responsible for his arrest, and the latter, who is Jack's uncle, are perceived by members of the reunion as substantially different political entities. As the novel progresses, however, the distinction resolves itself into one of family versus non-family. Early in the novel, for example, Aunt Birdie says of Curly: " 'Your votes is all he cares about. I swear he's too mean to live' " (p. 61). The opinion is borne out by Curly's initial failure to rescue Judge and Mrs. Moody (" 'I can't be late to my own fish-fry, can I? The sandbar's loading up with voters now,' " p. 152), and his manipulation of Jack's truck (" 'You traded this truck for the Foxtown votes. I see,' " p. 418).

Corrupt as Curly Stovall is revealed to be, however, he is politically indistinguishable from Homer Champion. Curly refuses to help Judge Moody, but it is Homer who reproves Jack for not behaving in the same way: " 'It was Judge Oscar Moody in the flesh, and you saved him.' Uncle Homer said. 'Wait till the rest of the voters hears about it' " (p. 82). The likeness of the two men is emphasized later in the narrative, when Aunt Birdie's judgment of Curly is echoed in Miss Beulah's words to her brother-in-law:

'My boy's keeping one end of
this man-foolishness from running
off with the other, with his bare
hands, and you just think about
Tuesday!' (p. 388)

The behavioral likeness of the two is paralleled by the similarity of their campaign slogans, printed on posters and nailed side by side on alternate trees (pp. 405, 411). That these similarities are the inherent similarities of a political family that links all office-seekers as "kin" is made explicit late in the novel:

> Now, election posters for races past and still to come embraced the bigger tree trunks. There were the faces of losers and winners, the forgotten and the remembered, still there together and looking like members of the same family. (p. 404)

The irony comes full circle late in the novel, however, when Ella Fay reveals a preference for Curly that may make her a bride. By marrying Curly, Ella Fay would be establishing him as "kin" to Homer Champion. The implications of the alliance are horrifying to Jack:

> 'Curly! Our battles'll be called off before they start! We'll all be one happy family!' Jack cried. 'I'll have to bow you a welcome in my own house where I can't lather you!' He pulled Curly to his feet and yelled in his face, 'With Uncle Homer out of the running, we'll even have to vote for you from now on!' (p. 412)

Choice of political affiliation here, as in The Ponder Heart, is essentially no choice at all, but rather a matter of loyalty to "kin."

The most politicized figure in the novel, however, is Miss Julia Mortimer. Like Miss Lottie Eckhart of The Golden Apples, Miss Julia Mortimer is a dynamic spinster who has attained the status of local, or geographic, legend.[22] Solely responsible for the education of Granny Vaughn's grandchildren and most of the Banner community, Miss Julia inspires both respect and fear not only in life, but also after death.[23] The importance of her legendary status is underscored by Miss Julia's ghostly presence throughout the narrative. Much of Losing Battles' two central books (Book 3, pp. 175-223; Book 4, pp. 227-308) reflect conversations by and about Miss Julia, her funeral procession occupies the novel's last pages (pp. 420-436), and her letter to Judge Moody provides its title (p. 307). Her legend is a composite portrait of indefatigable endurance (p. 242), strength (p. 235), and determination (pp. 236-9). As Uncle Dolphus puts it: "... she taught the generations. She was our cross to bear" (p. 240). A highly intelligent, extremely independent unmarried woman, Miss Julia's is a legend that runs counter to the Southern Romance. Although critics have labelled her the center of "reality"[24] or "nerve center"[25] in the novel, Miss Julia is actually an outsider to the emotional, or moral locus presented in <u>Losing Battles</u>. Her will to social reform undermines the mystique of the pastoral community. She is, to borrow Michael Kreyling's phrase, "the champion of the historical mind."[26] When Miss Julia brings milk to the children of Banner school, for example, her action is interpreted and reacted to as "relief" (p. 191): " 'Of course we had to pour ours right out on the ground,' said Aunt Nanny, 'Broadwees is as good as she is' " (p. 236).

Miss Julia's legendary counterpart, and the primary exemplar of the Southern Romance tradition within the novel, is Grandpa Vaughn. The image of religious zeal, "standing up in his long beard and looking ... over the Bible" (p. 50), Grandpa Vaughn was "the living example of a real, real Baptist" (p. 182). If Miss Julia's legend is social and political progress, Grandpa Vaughn's is familial and religious tradition:

> 'I'll never forget Grandpa at that last reunion,' said Uncle Curtis. 'Oh, he thundered! He preached at us from Romans and sent us all home still quaking for our sins.' (p. 183)

In his lifetime, Grandpa Vaughn was as much Banner's salvation as Miss Julia was its curse, and his absence from his wife's ninetieth birthday celebration marks the end of a tradition as significant as the end of social progress signalled by Miss Julia's death. Throughout the novel, the reunion reminds itself that Brother Bethune cannot equal Grandpa Vaughn (pp. 68, 177, 182-5, 191, 211, 236), and the repetition nearly renders the reunion as much a eulogy to the first year anniversary of her husband's death as a celebration of Granny Vaughn's birthday. As Miss Beulah puts it: " 'Oh, Grandpa Vaughn, I miss your presence!' " (p.

211). What Miss Beulah in fact misses is the way in
which Grandpa Vaughn filled his traditional role:
" 'None of this would have happened if Grandpa Vaughn
had this reunion in charge' " (p. 211). It is fitting,
therefore, that Grandpa Vaughn, the reunion's traditional core or central presence, had married Jack
Renfro and Gloria Short (p. 49) against the advice of
his ideological and legendary counterpart, Miss Julia
Mortimer (p. 249).

With the notion of a traditional core, we enter
the realm of family myth, where the historical (the
line) sustains the eternal mythical present (the circle) through what R. D. Laing has defined as a process
of "mapping."

> Between the truth that is
> called a lie, and the lie that is
> called the truth, lies the field
> of mystification, confusion con-
> founded into false clarity, where
> images and ideas we imagine and
> think are real, and that we must
> preserve, paralyse our imagination
> and our thinking.
> It seems to be done, in part,
> by a kind of projection. Each
> generation projects onto the next,
> elements derived from a product of
> at least three factors
> What was
> 1- projected onto it by
> prior generations
> 2- induced in it by prior
> generations, and
> 3- its response to this
> projection and induc-
> tion
> If I project an element $\underline{x}$
> from set A onto an element $\underline{y}$ of set
> B, and if we call the operation of
> projection or mapping $\emptyset_{27}$ then $\underline{y}$ is
> the image of $\underline{x}$ under $\emptyset$.

Brother Bethune can take Grandpa Vaughn's place at the
reunion, but he cannot replace the way in which Grandpa
Vaughn filled his role because the process of mapping
has not occurred. Mapping is the intergenerational
process that sustains a family's mythic configuration
over time. It is what allows the reunion to recreate

Rachel Sojourner in Gloria Short and Sam Dale Beecham
in Jack Jordan Renfro. Once the reunion has decided
that Gloria is Rachel's child, therefore, the likeness
between the two women becomes behavioral as well as
physical, and Rachel is mapped onto Gloria: " 'Yes,
your face is Rachel's entirely, and with all the wild
notions in it. Makes me remember how she used to vow
she was going clear to Ludlow some day, and live in
style' " (p. 268).

The mapping of Sam Dale Beecham onto Jack Jordan
Renfro is slightly more complex. Both are the favorite
sons of the matriarch Granny Vaughn (pp. 5, 328), who
were chased by Banner girls (" 'Every girl in Banner
was setting her cap for Sam Dale Beecham, and Jack went
through the same hard experience' ", p. 221) but maintained the strict moral code of the family: " 'Jack
Jordan Renfro never gave Banner community the first
cause for complaint! He'd treat a girl strictly the
way he's been everlastingly told,' " p. 263; " 'Sam
Dale wouldn't have got a girl in trouble and then gone
off and left her,' " p. 265) from which they are eventually taken (Jack by law, Sam Dale by death: " 'Let
him hop!' said Jack. 'Sam Dale wasn't hardly older
than I am now when they put him in that grave of
his,' " p. 427).[28] In the terms of family myth, Jack
is, as Brother Bethune knows, "the Prodigal Son" (p.
105) returned to replace Sam Dale in the reunion's configuration. Miss Beulah calls Jack " 'the nearest
thing to Sam Dale we've got today' " (p. 221), and the
identification is completed when Granny's call to Sam
Dale produces Jack instead: "Her hands reached for
Jack's face. Then a faint cry came, and her face,
right in his, broke all to pieces. 'But you're not Sam
Dale!' " (p. 308).

Mapping sustains family myth by subordinating
history to ritual. If, as we have said, the reunion is
a ritual drama taking place in the center of a circle,
then each family member is a character having a specific role or part to perform within the established cast
or configuration. If a role is vacated, then the cast
must fit a new member into that role through the
process Laing calls mapping. Jack's uniqueness apart
from Sam Dale is thus subordinated to myth, which is in
turn fed by actuality. In other words, historical myth
feeds ritual, which is in turn dependent upon the collaboration of family. As Laing puts it,

94

> The truth has to be expanded
> to sustain a family image. The
> family as a shared fantasy image
> is usually a container of some
> kind in which all members of the
> family feel themselves to be, and
> for which image all members of the
> family may feel each should sacri-
> fice themselves. Since this
> fantasy exists in so far as it is
> "in" everyone who shares "in" it,
> anyone who gives it up shatters
> the "family" in everyone else.[29]

Family myth is not only communal and solipsistic, but
also "central" (i.e., the zone of absolute reality).
In Welty's terms, "everything worth knowing in life is
in the family ... family relationships are the natural
basis of all other relationships."[30]

   Losing Battles is essentially a novel about what
belonging to a family signifies. The primary function
of family, and one colored by the mystique of the
pastoral community, is survival.[31] Miss Beulah is the
matriarchal successor of Granny Vaughn, and hers is the
voice that presides over family in Losing Battles. Her
explanations of the ritual are both defensive and protective of its familial configuration, and it is not
insignificant that they are most often directed toward
Aunt Cleo.[32] Late in the novel, for example, Miss
Beulah explains the necessity of family collaboration
to her sister-in-law as follows:

> 'By now you ought to know this is a
> strict, law-abiding, God-fearing,
> close-knit family, and everybody
> in it has always struggled the
> best we know how and we've all just
> tried to last as long as we can by
> sticking together.' (pp. 343-344)

For Miss Beulah, as for Granny Vaughn, both the living
and the dead are included in the reunion, not only
because family ties transcend time, but also because
the reunion takes place within the eternal mythical
present. Aunt Cleo's intimation, late in the novel,
that Granny is senile thus serves to isolate her as a
representative of historical time.

> 'Hey, don't she know the differ-
> ence yet? Who's alive and who's
> dead?' asked Aunt Cleo in a
> nurse's whisper.
>   'She knows we're all part of
> it together, or ought to be!' Miss
> Beulah cried, turning on her.
> 'That's more than some other peo-
> ple appear to have found out.' (p.
> 346)

Over the course of the novel, Miss Beulah not only
defends Granny Vaughn, but also Jack ("'Fiddle. My
boy'd get here today from anywhere he had to,' said
Miss Beulah loudly," p. 18) and Mr. Renfro (" 'He had
to show the reunion single-handed the world don't have
to go flying to pieces when the oldest son gives trouble,' " p. 66). And although she doesn't prevent
Gloria's initiation into the Beecham family, Miss
Beulah neither participates in it, nor deserts Gloria
after the event has taken place (p. 270).

Miss Beulah's defense of family is, however, most
often a statement of expectation -- that is, a
"scenario."[33] If Granny Vaughn, Miss Beulah, and
others have "induced" Jack to behave like Sam Dale
Beecham, then the composite of their mapping of Sam
Dale onto Jack is the family scenario for Jack's
behavior. In order to fulfill family expectations,
therefore, Jack must adhere to the family scenario
created for him. As Jack himself puts it, " 'nobody,
not even my wife, would have forgiven me for the rest
of my life if I hadn't showed up today' " (p. 195).
The expectation of Jack's return is established by
Granny Vaughn (" 'He can come right now,' " p. 5) and
Miss Beulah (" 'My boy's coming! My boy's coming!'
cried Miss Beulah. 'He's coming to surprise Granny --
we somehow just know it,' " p. 10) in the early pages
of the novel, and is sustained (" 'Bring him here to
me, will you?' said Granny. 'Don't keep Granny
waiting a good deal longer,' " p. 40) until Jack's
climactic arrival:

> ... Miss Beulah raced to Granny's
> side. The barking reached frantic
> pitch as a whirlwind of dust
> filled the space between the
> chinaberry trees. As even those
> chatterers on the back porch and
> those filling the house started up

> through the passage, the floor
> drummed and swayed, a pan dropped
> from its nail in the kitchen wall,
> and overhead even the tin of the
> roof seemed to quiver with a sound
> like all the family spoons set to
> jingling in their glass. (p.
> 71)³⁴

As his spectacular arrival indicates, Jack is the
reunion's emblem (the house itself is excited by his
arrival) with which the reunion per se begins (p. 14).
His arms are "like gates" that "the whole reunion at
once" tries to run in (p. 71), and his senses are the
record of family history:

> ... he leaned forward with his
> clear eyes fixed on the speaker as
> though what was now being said
> would never be said again or
> repeated by anybody else. (p. 79)

He has, quite simply, been selected family hero, and
the expectations that follow his return home pertain to
the scenario created for him by his family. Whether
the task is rescuing the Buick (" 'Jack Renfro will
find his own way,' said Miss Beulah. 'He's come along
too splendid to get himself licked in the morning,' "
p. 228), or the Renfro farm,

> 'And when Jack jumps out in those
> fields tomorrow, he'll resurrect
> something out of nothing. Don't
> you know he will?' cried Aunt
> Birdie.
> Aunt Nanny said, 'And Jack
> will butcher the hog. You'll tide
> yourselves over, one year more...
> 'You see, Judge Moody, and
> Mrs. Moody, now that Jack has come
> home to stay, everything's going
> to look up. It'll all be on his
> shoulders,' said Uncle Curtis.
> 'Trust him.' " (p. 326)

Jack's performance is one of "family duty" (p. 103):
" 'Jack wouldn't disappoint us, ' Aunt Nanny said. 'By
this time he wouldn't even know how' " (p. 180). In
telling Gloria that they have "the whole reunion behind
(them)" (p. 171) therefore, Jack is making a statement

about the strength of the family scenario and his role within it.

The expectations outlined for Jack in the family scenario are underscored by those outlined for his brother, Vaughn Renfro. Although Vaughn has been fulfilling his brother's duties at the farm since Jack left for Parchman ("doing what there was still nobody but him to do," p. 6), the family believes that Vaughn is incapable of replacing him:

> " 'Vaughn can't rob a hen's nest
> without Jack to tell him. Vaughn
> is not Jack, and never will be,'
> Miss Beulah confided at the top of
> her voice into the truck." (p.
> 402)

The family's belief that Vaughn cannot act without Jack is incorrect, as his discovery and return of the mortgages Jack had lost (p. 40) and the ease with which he rescues the school bus, "without the slightest fuss about it" (p. 364), illustrate. It is not insignificant, however, that these tasks are performed when Vaughn is alone, and that when summoned by the reunion he cannot act (p. 308). If Jack's scenario is that of family hero, then Vaughn's is that of family failure, and Vaughn cannot usurp the part of hero without proving his family members incorrect. If his mother calls him "contrary" (pp. 8, 12), then Vaughn must seem contrary in order to fit the scenario she has created for him: " 'He'll never be Jack,' she said. 'Says the wrong thing, does the wrong thing, doesn't do what I tell him. And perfectly satisfied to have you say so!' " (p. 12). Because he can neither alter the scenario nor his family's perceptions of him within it, Vaughn directs his anger toward Jack, the antagonist it provides for him. Vaughn predicts that Jack will be the last to arrive at the reunion (p. 8), tells Aunt Birdie he wouldn't care if his brother failed to arrive at the reunion until the next day (p. 11), confides to the darkness that " 'without Jack, nothing would be no trouble at all' " (p. 364), and blames the loss of the hay to his having been made " ' to wait on Jack' " (p. 373). Finally, when Jack does return, Vaughn ceremonially fights him with dried corn stalk swords (p. 72). Thus, caught both by the legend of his namesake on the one hand and the heroism of his brother on the other, Vaughn lives in the double-bind of family: " 'It's no blooming fair,' said Vaughn, accepting it" (p. 398).

The uncontested hero of Losing Battles, Jack is as much the product as he is the hope of the reunion, and its familial values are his values.[35] When Homer Champion and Curly Stovall take him to Parchman, for example, it is Curly whom Jack struggles against out of respect for Homer, who is married to Mr. Renfro's sister Auntie Fay (p. 41). Charlie Roy Hugg similarly escapes Jack's anger by virtue of being "kin" to Aycock Comfort's mother (p. 51), and Jack is even capable of treating Curly as a brother-in-law should the need arise (p. 412). Jack understands that his obligation to the reunion (" 'He made a monkey out of you. Now you can make a monkey out of him. ... That's all the reunion is asking of you,' " p. 86) is necessary because a joke on Jack is a "joke on the whole reunion" (p. 83). As he explains it to Gloria,

> '... I'm beholden to the reunion to keep it running on a smooth track today, for Granny's birthday to be worth her living to see. For Mama's chickens not to go wasted, and for all of 'em that's traveled through dust not to go home disappointed. It's up to me to meet that Judge, Possum, sing him my name out loud and clear, and leave him in as good a ditch as the one he had before I saved him. That's all.' (p. 112)

Aunt Birdie validates the truth of his perception as Jack leaves for Banner Top: " 'Even if the reunion was to stop this minute, it would have been worth coming through the dust for' " (p. 94). Once Judge Moody swerves the Buick to avoid colliding with Gloria and Lady May, however, Jack's allegiance to the reunion is superseded by his duty to the Judge, which takes the form of rescuing Mrs. Moody's car from Banner Top without the help of any "outsiders" (pp. 125, 128, 134, 153-4).

Jack's obligation to Judge Moody, like that to the reunion, is connected to his role within the family, and in Losing Battles the symbol of family is the wedding ring. Jack's initial sentencing had, in fact, resulted from his gallant attempt to retrieve the ring belonging to Granny Vaughn's daughter Ellen (p. 26), an action appropriately perceived by the reunion as a matter of family honor rather than of stealing.[36] Aunt

Nanny calls the wedding ring "the most precious trea-
sure there is" (p. 24), and it is this "precious gold
band, the only one like it in Christendom" (p. 62) that
begins Jack's heroic quest or, as Miss Beulah puts it,
" 'what he went to all the trouble for' " (p. 33).
Gloria is connected to the ring by hair that is
"wedding-ring gold" (p. 47), a color so bright that it
not only prevents Aycock from looking straight at her,
but also turns his ears gold (p. 116). Miss Beulah's
wedding ring, as inseparable from her day-to-day living
presence (p. 219) as Ellen's is from the collective
past of family history, indicates a perpetuation of the
cyclic concerns of the reunion. As Miss Beulah says
mid-way through the novel, " 'It's the same gold ring,
and all the one sad story' " (p. 219).

Before its loss, Ellen's ring had been kept in the
Vaughn Bible, a repository of family history not unlike
the Shellmound library of <u>Delta Wedding</u>.

> She dwelt for a moment over
> the angel-decorated roster of
> births and deaths set down in
> various hands, then lifted and wet
> her finger and began turning
> systematically through her Bible -
> -not as though she needed to hunt
> for what she wanted but as though
> she were coming to it in her own
> way. Those nearest her saw the
> lock of Ellen's hair when it went
> by in Chronicles, pale as silk.
> Deep in the crease of First Thes-
> salonians lay Grandpa's specta-
> cles. Granny poked them free and
> put them on top of hers. Here came
> the ribbon that had held Ellen's
> ring, like a pressed flower stem
> without its flower. Then she
> turned one more page and drew out
> what looked like a brownish post-
> card. It had lain in its place so
> long that it had printed the page
> brown too, with a pattern like
> moire. (p. 266)

The Vaughn Bible is a book within a book, a history
that links the familial and the sacred in much the same
way as the reunion links history and myth. Vaughn
Renfro, more than any other character in <u>Losing</u>

Battles, feels the presence of history in myth the night the century plant blooms. Riding Bet in the darkness, Vaughn hears "every sound going on, repeating itself, increasing, as if it were being recollected by loud night talking to itself" (p. 363). The night is the reverberation of the day, and the day is the eternal mythical present that blurs distinctions between the living and the dead, the past and the present. When Vaughn re-enters the barn, therefore, it is filled with "the electrical memory of Dan the horse, the upper regions full of Grandpa Vaughn's prayers" (p. 367). The farm is thus the place where history and myth intersect in the ritual of reunion. In Mircea Eliade's terms, "nature undergoes a transformation from the very fact of the kratophany of hierophany, and emerges from it charged with myth."[37] In other words, place is the composite of its history illuminated by ritual action. As Welty puts it in "Some Notes on River Country," "a place that ever was lived in is like a fire that never goes out."[38] Although the coals are always live, it is ritual that brings them to flame. Miss Beulah's wedding photo ("the only picture that ever was made of our whole family") thus gains mythic significance when the configuration is repeated in a ritual that juxtaposes time and place.

> The earlier company had lined up three deep that day on the front porch and steps of this house where they themselves were now. They stood then in April light: the house stood dark, roof and all, as a woodsy mountain behind the water-splash of the bride.
> (p. 327)

The ghostly face of Sam Dale Beecham holds the other faces at both sides of the photograph like a pair of bookends (p. 328), its very ghostliness not only suggestive of his death the following year, but also of his importance to a family that maps him onto Jack Jordan Renfro one generation later.[39] The quilt Granny Vaughn receives as a birthday present similarly confounds time and place through ritual. the quilt's pattern, "The Delectable Mountains," is here as in Delta Wedding not only an indicator of the region in which it was made (the upstate hill country of Mississippi),[40] but also of the tradition that produced it. Thus, the quilt, like the photograph, synthesizes time and place through the collaboration of family in ritual action. Jack senses this connection once when he takes Gloria and Lady May to Banner Top (pp. 101-3), and again later when he recognizes that the meaning of prison is removal from home, the place where family history and myth intersect: " 'I reckon for every spot there is, there's somebody in the pen going homesick for it' " (p. 116).

As in Delta Wedding and The Ponder Heart, voluntarily leaving home is here a sign of betrayal. Uncle Homer is never "forgiven" (p. 77) for moving to Southern Mississippi; Jack does not forgive Judge Moody for sending him to Parchman (p. 211) even though his family does (p. 209). Uncle Noah Webster is still "Benedict Arnold" (p. 194) to Granny Vaughn even though he was the last to leave her, and the threat of losing Jack, Gloria, and Lady May to Alabama is, to Uncle Curtis, tantamount to their deaths: " 'There ain't no end, it looks like, to what you can lose and still go on living ' " (p. 321). The deepest understanding of this sense of loss is attributed to Gloria.

> And so she convinced him that
> there is only one way of depriving
> the ones you love -- taking your
> living presence away from theirs;
> that no one alive has ever
> deserved such punishment, although
> maybe the dead do; and that no one
> alive can ever in honor forgive
> that wrong, which outshines shame,
> and is not to be forgiven until it
> has been righted. (p. 362)

Earlier in the novel, however, it was Gloria who had asked Jack, " 'When will we move to ourselves?' " (p. 111).

A "little nobody from out of nowhere" (p. 60), Gloria's attitude toward family is paradoxical. Although she perceives herself, her husband, and her child as a family, she does not acknowledge belonging to the extended family within which hers is set. To Gloria, the reunion is a burden, a destructive ritual that enmeshes and suffocates her husband: " 'The most they ever do for you is brag on you' " (p. 137). Retrieving Ellen's ring, therefore, is neither viewed by Gloria as stealing nor seen as an act of family honor, but is rather understood as a manifestation of home ties: " 'Your honor, I'm here to tell you Jack

Renfro's case in two words -- home ties. Jack Renfro has got family piled all over him' " (p. 163). Her desire to move her family off the Renfro farm is a desire to extricate Jack from the eternal mythical present contained in place.

> 'Oh, if we just had a little
> house to ourselves, no bigger than
> our reach right now,' she whis-
> pered. 'And nobody could ever
> find us! But everybody finds us.
> Living or dead.' (p. 171)[41]

What Gloria wants, in effect, is, as she tells the reunion, " 'to save him! From everybody I see this minute!' " (pp. 198, 320).

It is ironic, therefore, that the reunion not only reveals Gloria's relationship to Rachel Sojourner, but also her possible connection to Sam Dale Beecham, alliances that together would create family ties more extensive than those of Jack himself: " 'One way or other, I'm kin to everybody in Banner' " (p. 313).[42] Despite these possible kinships, Gloria not only refuses to alter her perception of Jack's family (" 'not for all the tea in China,' " p. 360), but also to change the way in which she sees herself: " 'I'm here to be nobody but myself, Mrs. Gloria Renfro, and have nothing to do with the old dead past' " (pp. 361, 315). That Gloria similarly wishes to remain an orphan from the "family" of teachers traveling to pay their respects to Miss Julia Mortimer (" 'You're still one of us, Gloria Short,' " p. 158) is evident by her decision to remain with Jack and Lady May despite their attempts to persuade her otherwise.

Leaving one's place of birth is not only a be-trayal of family, but also a betrayal of origin, or identity. As we have said, family expects its members to maintain a connection between identity and place (what McMillen calls "home"). As in Delta Wedding and The Ponder Heart, identity informs place (that is, place gains significance from identity: " 'Jack Renfro might just as well have been a boy was never heard of around here for the treatment he got from you in Ludlow,' " p. 210) which, in turn, defines identity (the cast of characters which prefaces the novel lists family by town). It is this interdependence of iden-tity and place that constitutes point of view. In "Place in Fiction," Welty observes that "it is by

103

knowing where you stand that you grow able to judge
where you are."[43] If "where you stand" can be defined
as the connection between place and identity, then
"where you are" can signify point of view, the relationship between "where you stand" and the rest of the
world. Gloria's adamant rejection of both name and
place (" 'I'm an orphan, sir ... and Banner is not my
home,' " p. 106), for example, enables her to disown
the Vaughn-Beecham-Renfro point of view as it surfaces
in the reunion. By disavowing identity and place,
Gloria can project where she is as a better place than
where she happens to find herself. Gloria's point of
view confounds Miss Beulah, to whom family is (in terms
of ritual) sacred:

> 'She's from the Ludlow Pres-
> byterian Orphan Asylum, if you
> want to hear it exactly,' said
> Miss Beulah. 'And how she turns
> all that around into something to
> be conceited about is a little bit
> more than I can tell you.' (pp.
> 60-1)

Gloria's point of view, like that of Robbie Reid in
Delta Wedding, is antithetical to that of the family.[44]
She can not be "read," much to Miss Beulah's dismay
(pp. 69, 94), and enjoys being a mystery to the family
with which she lives (pp. 251-2): " 'Gloria Short! I
declare but you're turning out to be a little question
mark!' " (p. 197). It is, in fact, the lack of identity signalled in Gloria's naming and assigned date of
birth (April Fool's Day, p. 255) that is her signature
in the novel, making her as much an object of awe to
the reunion as she is a source of bewilderment. Her
ability to look " 'cooler and cleaner than you do' "
(p. 14), her aloofness (p. 19), the fact that " 'she
can roll up her hair in the dark' " (p. 69), and that
she has won the state spelling match (p. 242), and her
walk ("as though small bells had been hung, without her
permission, on her shoulders, hips, breasts, even
elbows, tinkling only just out of ears' range," p. 73)
all serve to enhance Gloria's puzzling beauty.

Gloria is not the only character in Losing Battles
whose name comprises a signature of identity. Early in
the novel, for example, Curly Stovall is explained to
Aunt Cleo through an encapsulating portrait the accu-
racy of which is immediately confirmed by Aunt Nanny:

'Tell what he's like, quick,'
said Aunt Birdie.
'He's great big and has little bitty eyes!' came the voice of
Ella Fay from where she was
pulling honeysuckle off the cow
shed. 'Baseball cap and side-
burns!'
'She's got it! Feel like I
can see him coming right this
minute,' said Aunt Nanny, hitching
forward in her rocker. (p. 23)

Charlie Roy Hugg is similarly evoked for Aunt Cleo
through a verbal shorthand

'What's his style?'
'Drunk and two pistols.
Makes his wife answer the phone.'

that she, in turn, immediately understands: " 'We got
his twin in Piney' " (p. 51). Aycock Comfort (" 'He's
a Banner boy and a friend of Jack's. What's wrong with
him is he ain't Jack,' " p. 36), Miss Pet Hanks
(" 'Miss Pet Hanks is Central in Medley,' " p. 34),
Aunt Cleo (" 'a settled white Christian lady with no
home ties and drawing a pension,' " p. 76), Willie
Trimble (" 'He's such an old bachelor that the way he
cleans out his fireplace is to carry the ashes through
the house, shovel-load at a time, and dump 'em out
through the front door,' " p. 80), Ora Stovall
(" 'weigh more than I should, never married, but know
how to meet the public, keep up with what's going
on,' " p. 381), Sam Dale Beecham (" 'Handsomer than
Dolphus ever was, sunnier than Noah Webster, smarter
than Percy, more home-loving than Curtis, more quiet-
spoken than Nathan, and could let you have a tune
quicker and truer than all the rest put together,' " p.
221), and Uncle Nathan (" 'Walking cane! And a straw
hat with a stripey band on it. A flowing tie!,' " p.
329) are all reduced to the verbal shorthand of signature.

Uncle Percy's voice (p. 11) and Miss Lexie's spinsterhood (p. 16) are as much familiar identification
marks as they are simple facts, and serve to summarize
their owners with a force as great as Uncle Nathan's
religious signs (p. 124) and Mr. Renfro's new tin roof
(p. 90) do theirs. Banner itself is the proud signature that its name suggests, and it is not insignif-

icant that Dearman, who " 'followed the tracks' " into
Banner to found a sawmill and depart following the
railroad that brought him (pp. 341-2), is from
Manifest, Mississippi -- a name that echoes the theory
of Manifest Destiny he exemplifies. Miss Julia
Mortimer's name similarly reinforces the linear, or
historical point of view[45] that runs counter to the
reunion's cyclic pattern, while Jack's has a traditional association with folktale.[46] Even the bois d'
arc tree, named Billy Vaughn's Switch by the old-
timers, links the beginnings of the Vaughn-Beecham-
Renfro family with the theme of endurance against
history: "The tree looked a veteran of all the old
blows, a survivor" (p. 181).[47]

One way in which family survives in Losing Battles
is through the acceptance of narrator or story-teller
as authority. The "shared family image" that defines
family myth is sustained through the language of its
members, who are neither confronted with errors in, nor
expected to defend opinions about, what they say during
the reunion. Thus Granny Vaughn can claim that she is
"a hundred today" (p. 5) although she is actually
ninety, Brother Bethune can confuse the facts of
Grandpa Vaughn's death (p. 183), and Gloria can be pro-
claimed a Beecham on speculation (" "Say Beecham!' they
ordered her, close to her ear," p. 269). Linked
together, the incidents of family myth form narration.
Uncle Percy's narration of events leading to Jack's
sentencing (pp. 21, 22-39, 64, 146) is similarly given
the credence of heroic myth by his listeners within the
reunion, and the novel as a whole forms an example of
oral tradition that relies not only upon the story, but
also upon the validity of its teller.[48] Like The
Ponder Heart, therefore, Losing Battles is a novel
controlled by voices. Here, however, the voices
collaborate to create and sustain a family myth that
is, after all, a composite. As Miss Beulah says, it's
" 'all the one sad story. ... You didn't hear but the
Renfro part this morning' " (p. 219).

Talk is the medium of the reunion, and one of its
forms is news. Miss Pet Hanks, like Eva Sistrunk of
The Ponder Heart, listens to the town's news over her
telephone (p. 34), news of other towns is Jack's plea-
sure at Parchman (p. 116) just as news about home is
his welcome (p. 113), and family news is regarded as
family business (pp. 55-6) that even Gloria need not
tell (pp. 48, 69). News has its appropriate teller,
and Etoyle is perceived by the family as an unreliable

narrator because she consistently "embroiders" her
stories (p. 34) not to serve family myth, but rather to
sensationalize.

> 'And Etoyle said Homer warned
> him before they started that if he
> give any more trouble resisting
> arrest he'd get a bullet ploughed
> through his leg.'
> 'Etoyle embroiders.' (p. 42)

Gloria's female relations ceremonially chant instruc-
tions to her the day of Jack's arrival with an authority not unlike that of the Greek dramatic chorus
(" 'Sit still, Sister Gloria, keep your hands folded,
don't let your dress get dirty ...,' " pp. 15, 19-20),
and the aunts similarly repeat and reinforce one
another with a chorus-like precision.

> 'Pore Jack! How he made it up
> that first hill is over and beyond
> my comprehension,' said Aunt
> Nanny.
> 'Pore Jack! It's just a
> wonder he didn't fall flat on his
> face, once and for all,' said Aunt
> Beck. (p. 31)

Echoing one another in speech (p. 66) and action (pp.
219, 262, 269), the aunts, and occasionally the reunion
as a whole (pp. 230, 234, 316), provide the context
within which the eternal mythical present can surface
by forming a composite narrative authority, a consist-
ent voice that is the voice of the reunion itself.

In a sense, the reunion is the celebration of
verbal over written authority. Gloria's past, for
example, is reconstructed out of speculation, hearsay,
and memory and, once articulated, is validated by the
reunion (" 'We told you who you are. Ain't you even
going to say thank you?' " p. 268). If the reunion is
empowered to speak them into existence, however, Gloria
is able to will her parents away: " "I won't be a
Beecham!' " (p. 265). Ultimately, however, it is
Granny Vaughn who is given the option of determining
whether or not the reunion will have Sam Dale be
Gloria's father: " 'Granny, which would you rather?
Keep Sam Dale perfect, or let him be a father after
all?' " (p. 345). Although Judge Moody believes that
" 'you can't change what's happened by taking a voice

vote on it' " (p. 345), he is an outsider, and representative of the world of linear, or historical, time and therefore cannot comprehend the multiple interpretations of event contained in the eternal mythical present. The way in which Gloria's past is resolved in the eternal mythical present is to be left a matter of individual selection between two equally true solutions.

> 'You missed things,' called Auntie Fay serenely, as the Champions' chicken van bounced into the yard and stopped under a moonstruck fall of dust. 'Gloria's born a Beecham, she's Sam Dale's child -- that's the best surprise that was brought us. She's here tonight as one of the family twice over. -- Oh no she isn't! -- Well, believe what you want to.' (p. 336)

Auntie Fay's serenity is that of narrative authority operating within the eternal mythical present.

In <u>Losing Battles</u>, narrative authority is the only authority. As Judge Moody realizes, the evidence and fact inherent to written records were destroyed the day the courthouse burned: " 'There's no written proof left that any of us at all are alive here tonight' " (p. 322). Judge Moody's despair is that of Miss Julia Mortimer, for whom written " 'words, just words, was getting to be something good enough to eat' " (p. 282). Miss Julie Mortimer -- whose identity is encapsulated both in the letter she writes to Judge Moody (pp. 297-8) and in her will (pp. 289-92) and Judge Moody himself are two of the novel's representatives of the historical point of view. When Judge Moody opens Miss Julia Mortimer's letter, therefore, the reunion doesn't want to hear the written record of her words (pp. 297-9), but rather his spoken version of it: "I can't understand it when he reads it to us. Can't he just tell it?' " (p. 298). In reading her letter, Judge Moody is exposing how Miss Julia Mortimer felt at a given point in her life -- that is, he's reading <u>her</u>. To Gloria, and the rest of the reunion, however, " 'people don't want to be read like books' " (p. 432). What people <u>do</u> want is to create the eternal mythical present through talk. Without records, talk is the only way in which

one's existence is affirmed: Without talk, there is
nothing (pp. 312, 340).

Talk is, among other things, the verbal record of
event. In an interview for the Jackson Daily News
(April 5, 1970), Welty explained that she wanted "to
show everything outwardly if I could, rather than
writing about what people were thinking, I wanted to
show it in word and action." Event, like language,
surfaces within the eternal mythical present of the
reunion. Jack Jordan Renfro can thus be both surprised
by some events of the past (that his truck now belongs
to Curly Stovall, pp. 67, 88, 144; that Grandpa Vaughn
has died, p. 69; that his horse has been sold, p. 89)
and not surprised by others (his daughter's existence
and name, pp. 91-2). Jack's surprises, like Brother
Bethune's family history (pp.   178-85) share the
immediacy of event through the structure of the
reunion. As Mr. Renfro puts it, " 'It's all part of
the reunion. We got to live it out, son' " (p. 211).
Although the ritual of the reunion partakes of the
eternal mythical present, however, the land's cycle and
the cycle of day and night produce their own events:
rain ruins the hay (p. 373), darkness comes (p. 311),
and only flux is a certainty.

> As they sang, the tree over
> them, Billy Vaughn's Switch, with
> its ever-spinning leaves all
> light-points at this hour, looked
> bright as a river, and the tables
> might have been a little train of
> barges it was carrying with it,
> moving slowly downstream. Brother
> Bethune's gun, still resting
> against the trunk, was travelling
> too, and nothing at all was unmov-
> able, or empowered to hold the
> scene still fixed or stake the
> reunion there. (p. 223)

The implications of flux are those of losing time, and
in Losing Battles, losing time is equal to losing one's
memory of oneself. The photograph of Miss Beulah's
wedding is startling because it illustrates the
disjunction between the eternal mythical present and
historical time. As Aunt Birdie puts it, " 'I always
forget what tricks time likes to play' " (p. 329).
What Aunt Birdie, in fact, forgets is that she has lost
the memory of herself over time. Granny senses the

same loss after she forgets having received her birthday presents (pp. 287-8). Although the distance
between the event and the loss of its memory is shorter
for Granny than for Aunt Birdie, the process is the
same. What each woman perceives in the loss of memory
is the intrusion of the historical into the mythic --
the circle bending to the line. Despite the claims of
the reunion, therefore, it is inevitable that its hero,
Jack, be lost for a time in sleep: "Everything love
had sworn and done seemed to be already gone from him.
Even its memory was a measure away from him" (p. 362).

If the reunion is the eternal mythical present,
then it is a composite of the past extending into the
future. For the reunion, past and future are contained
in the present precisely because the present is both
eternal and mythic. The equipoise of Mrs. Moody's
Buick resting on Banner Top illustrates perfectly this
sense of suspended time, the moment which is itself the
culmination of all that has gone before it.

> 'I suppose you're happy,'
> Mrs. Moody said to her husband.
> 'There it is. On that ledge.'
> 'It brings some relief,' he
> said. 'Of course it's temporary.'
> 'It looks to me just a whole
> lot like it's permanent,' she told
> him. (p. 393)

The equipoise of the Buick is suspended time -- the
temporary moment that itself seems permanent. After
the moment passes, however, what is left is starting
over. When the cyclone destroys half of Banner, therefore, " 'it made just another case of having to start
over' " (p. 239). Miss Julia Mortimer's advice to
Uncle Nathan (" '... even when there's nothing left to
hope for, you can start again from there,' " p. 344) is
similarly the only advice she can give herself when the
library is destroyed by rain (p. 274), and Jack's
return is, on its broadest level, a like beginning:
" 'It's a start,' said Jack. Then he swung around.
'But for right now, Gloria, there's a lot of doing I
got to catch up with at home' " (p. 435). The pattern
of the book is itself a movement from the beginning of
one day (pp. 3-93: morning) to the beginning of another
(pp. 371-436: morning), full of more promise than the
first: " 'And when Jack jumps out in those fields
tomorrow, he'll resurrect something out of nothing.
Don't you know he will?' " (p. 326).

It at first seems paradoxical that much of the reunion is spent in waiting. Although it primarily waits for Jack's arrivals from Parchman and Banner Top (pp. 8, 10, 14, 20, 40, 93, 115, 164, 170), the reunion also waits for the century plant to bloom (" 'Well, I reckon that's what you've all been waiting for,' " p. 349), and even for itself (" 'You'll have to wait for next year,' " p. 355). In the eternal mythical present, movement has its own cycle. Rather than precipitating events, one waits for them. It is pointless to seek a wrecker for her Buick because, as Mrs. Moody tells her husband, " 'it comes without being called, Judge' " (p. 414). The ritual of myth is circular, and circles are repetitive. It is because Jack has left the family, therefore, that he must return to complete the journey cycle that his leaving has begun (" 'Birdie, Jack hasn't reached the table yet. Everything in its time,' " p. 177), and even Willie Trimble knows that the best way of finding what one is looking for is by staying put: " 'Stand still: your answer always comes along' " (p. 154). The philosophy is a reassuring one in that it frees the individual from a responsibility to time and event. The reunion waits for, and is lulled by, Brother Bethune's forgiveness of Judge Moody (p. 108), and Jack's sentence at Parchman is itself a period of limbo that frees the reunion from the responsibility of action: " '... what it left us with, after Jack got hauled to the pen, was a peaceful feeling of having something to wait for' " (p. 205). What the reunion waits for is completion of the cycle that sent Jack away in the first place. What it doesn't realize, however, is that the cycle may end unexpectedly in the marriage of Curly Stovall and Ella Fay Renfro (p. 412).

The reunion's waiting is the fatalistic waiting of both the mythic and the natural landscape. In the former (the eternal mythical present) waiting is "peaceful" because its reward (completion) is inevitable; in the latter, waiting is simply what happens between periods of movement. In the natural landscape, the bed of pinestraw waits for Jack and Gloria (p. 171), the Methodist and Baptist churches each "outwait the other" as if to "see which would fall first" (p. 406), the borrowed tables wait for Jack to return them after the reunion (p. 426), and the Buick waits as patiently to be rescued (pp. 150, 384) as its spectators wait to witness the event (pp. 132, 396).

111

Outside the eternal mythical present, however, waiting becomes, as Miss Beulah knows, "standing it"; " 'After they've all gone home, Ralph, and the children's in bed, that's what's left. Standing it' " (p. 360). It is this kind of waiting, waiting inside historical time, that has been Gloria's hardship (p. 19), and what she, like Miss Beulah before her (p. 354), tries to teach her child: " 'Learn to wait' " (p. 47). To Gloria, the surprises Jack receives are the painful byproducts of historical time -- a time frame that does not, according to Gloria, stop with the reunion:

> '... you can't just prance back
> like this and take it for granted
> that all you have to do is come
> home -- and life will go on like
> before, or even better.' (p. 109)

It is, in fact, Gloria's belief that " 'life don't just stop' " (pp. 113, 144) either for her husband or for the reunion that insures the perpetuation of Jack's heroic scenario. That is, events that occur in Jack's absence demand (in terms of his role within the family) his presence to be corrected. If, however, the projected fight with Curly Stovall (for example) becomes instead a marriage between the two families, then Jack must find new trials through which to reassert his familial identity. Although the process is, as Miss Beulah recognizes, " 'a heap more trouble! For everybody!' " (p. 63), she also recognizes its importance. The hero must have an arena in which to exercise his heroism and, in Losing Battles, the arena is Banner. Well immersed in his rescue of Mrs. Moody's car, Jack states the irony of his position: " I'm the Good Samaritan! And I've been it just about all day!' " (p. 149). In a sense, Jack's battles must be losing in order for him to maintain heroic combat. The hero is only a hero if there is a battle, and here, the existence of the battle is more significant than its outcome.

Event has another ironic component, however, and one that becomes ominous as the novel progresses. The possibilities of incest between Jack and Gloria Renfro are the result of mapping. It is because Gloria is as much a mystery as was her mother, Rachel Sojourner, that her history is open to induction by the reunion. In Laing's terms, "through these labyrinthine paths, the dream or nightmare of one generation comes to be

enacted generations later, too late to be true."[49] If
the reunion is guilty of mapping the nightmare of
Rachel's history onto Gloria, then Gloria aids the
process by refusing to listen to her oracle, Miss Julia
Mortimer.

> 'I said it suited me all
> right kept dark the way it was. I
> didn't mind being a mystery -- I
> was used to it. And if I was born
> a mystery, I'd be married a
> mystery.' (p. 251)

It is inevitable, therefore, that in seeking to escape
her past, Gloria, like Oedipus, should be confronted by
it:

> 'And I thought when I came to
> Banner to teach my first school, I
> was going forth into the world,'
> said Gloria.
> 'Instead, you was coming
> right back to where you started
> from,' said Aunt Birdie. 'Just as
> dangerous as a little walking
> stick of dynamite.' (p. 319)

In terms of family myth, Gloria's is an extension of
her mother's story, and both stories exist in the eternal mythical present. Together, the stories form a
cycle remininscent of the wedding band, but here the
return is potentially as tragic as that of Oedipus:

> 'All the time Jack took, all the
> load he shouldered, and all the
> trouble he went to, even blacken-
> ing his name going to Parchman,
> was to marry his own cousin and
> have Judge Moody come back and
> open the door so Curly Stovall
> could walk in the house and arrest
> him all over again.' (p. 318)

The primary ironies of Gloria's situation not only
revolve around her possible relation to a family and
town that she despises, but also concern that family's
response to the thought of incest. The reaction of
Miss Beulah (" 'I can die happy! Can't I?,' " p. 268)
precedes Gloria's mock initiation into the Beecham
family, and serves to illuminate the extent to which

113

that family's ego- and ethnocentricity will take it.
For Gloria's possible blood kinship to her husband is
only regretted by the reunion when Judge Moody raises
the question of its illegality (p. 321). In this way,
the threat of physical incest reveals what Andrew Lytle
has called "the incest of the spirit"[50] that is at the
very heart of the reunion. The quest to discover
Gloria's identity thus results in a revelation of
familial identity made ironic by that family's
inability to perceive its own insights.

Unlike the reunion, Judge Moody understands what
insight his journey of discovery affords. Like
Gloria's, Judge Moody's journey takes him directly back
to Banner: " 'Why we're right back in mortal sight of
that!' Mrs. Moody's face, looking at the way they'd
come, became mapped in pink. 'For all we've tra-
velled!' " (p. 410). Judge Moody's arrival in Banner
is the product of a chain of accidents: " '... I lost
my own way on Boone County roads for the first time I
can remember. I could almost believe I'd been
maneuvered here' " (p. 303). Like the Natchez Trace of
The Robber Bridegroom, the roads of Banner are the
medium through which Judge Moody loses his way in order
to find himself:

> In a voice so still and so
> stubborn that he might have been
> speaking to himself alone, Judge
> Moody said, 'Nothing wrong. Only
> I don't care quite the same about
> living as I did this morning.' (p.
> 307)

One way in which to fully understand the teachings of
Miss Julia Mortimer is to return to those she attempted
to teach. The return in fact completes two cycles:
Judge Moody's return to his mentor, and the conclusion
of Miss Julia Mortimer's frustrated attempt to teach
(revealed through her letter and will). Thus, for
Judge Moody Miss Julia's funeral is the symbolic and
literal arrival at the realization of loss. The
feeling of not caring "quite the same about living"
after his experience as before it that is Judge Moody's
insight is mirrored by that of Gloria, who, if she
still believes the future will be better than the past,
at least acknowledges her symbolic and literal isolation in kinship: "... she looked out to see the
distance, but beyond the bright porch she couldn't see
anything at all" (p. 320).

114

Judge Moody's journey, like Miss Julia
Mortimer's, is primarily linguistic. Judge Moody comes
to terms with his feeling for Miss Julia Mortimer, who
in turn comes to terms with hers for the Banner
community, through language. As in The Ponder Heart,
the ability of language to order chaos is profound.
Uncle Noah Webster's refrain (" 'that's what we're
doing -- bringing him,' " pp. 32, 40) emphasizes the
ability of family and language to produce Jack from
Parchman: " 'Jack Jordan Renfro,' announced Miss Lexie
to the company. 'Well: you brought him' " (p. 71; pp.
352, 354). The collaboration of family and language
constitutes a specialized "grammar." As Edward Sapir
defines it, grammar is "a generalized expression of the
feeling that analogous concepts and relations are most
conveniently symbolized in analogous forms."[51] Miss
Lexie's definition of the family as an unbroken circle
(p. 18) is therefore a significant grammatical expression because it reinforces linguistically the visual
concept of the reunion as a circle. If language
defines the way in which the reunion perceives itself,
then Gloria's comment to Miss Julia Mortimer -- "...
'the family was still trying to scrape a living from
this old farm, the circle still unbroken, nine mouths
to feed ...' " (p. 249) -- is as telling as Miss
Lexie's because it identifies her as part of the
Vaughn-Beecham-Renfro family.

Grammar allows for the sentence, and the sentence,
again to quote Sapir, "is the outgrowth of historical
and of unreasoning psychological forces rather than of
a logical synthesis of elements that have been clearly
grasped in their individuality."[52] In Losing Battles,
stories are thus the constructs produced by sentences
partaking of a family grammar.[53] Although they may
change according to the teller, stories are basically
fixed within the family because the grammar out of
which they are built is traditional. It is therefore
somewhat arbitrary that Brother Bethune recite the
family history, because whoever recites it will be
speaking out of the same vocabulary. In this sense,
language is as predictable, or ritualistic, a part of[54]
the reunion as are the hymn and the song. When
language is unpredictable, it is rendered meaningless.
The clergyman presiding over Miss Julia Mortimer's
funeral, for example, is an outsider and therefore
cannot speak through the family grammar: "Then the
priest opened his mouth and words came out --unfamiliar
in Banner Cemetery, not a one of them understood" (p.
430).

115

It is through the process of talk that language orders chaos. Throughout the novel, various member of the reunion are encouraged to tell its stories (p. 216, 241, 427), all of which resound in the silence of the night that follows it -- "all telling it -- bragging, lying, singing, pretending, protesting, swearing everything into being, swearing everything away -- but telling it" (p. 363). "Telling it" validates one's memory and perception because it is a way of knowing. Brother Bethune's recognition of Jack confirms his own sense of self by ordering the unfamiliar configuration before him:

> 'Just stand still. I want you
> folks to keep me company til I can
> tell you who you are.' (p. 104)
>
> 'It's the Prodigal Son.' (p. 105)

Jack's insistence on confronting Judge Moody with his identity (" 'My name is Jack Jordan Renfro,' " p. 163) the reunion's desire to name Gloria's mother (p. 253), Miss Pet Hanks' wish to assign an identity to Gloria's own fear that incest will cancel her baby's name (pp. 316-7), the settlers' need to name place (p. 355), and Jack's singing, loud enough so that "all Banner could hear him and know who he was" (p. 436) -- all serve to familiarize the unfamiliar, to order an otherwise chaotic world. The question " 'can't conversation ever cease?" (p. 390) is thus existential. Conversation cannot cease as long as the need to order chaos, and its corollary, the need to perpetuate family myth, are answered by it.

When language does not order chaos, when it runs counter to family myth, then knowing becomes as dangerous as silence itself. Miss Beulah's fear in pursuing Gloria's identity (" 'Let's stop before we get started. Let's perish the whole idea,' " p. 265) is the fear that language can destroy as well as create. Her disclosure of Sam Dale's possible impotence (" 'I guess I'm going to have to tell it,' " p. 323), for example, sacrifices one bit of family myth (Sam Dale's perfection) to preserve another (that Jack and Gloria are not blood relations). Miss Julia Mortimer's insistence that Judge Moody will "have to hear the story" (Gloria's) she wishes to tell him (p. 300), and Judge Moody's relation of that story to an unwilling reunion (" 'I wish we didn't have to hear it,' " p. 299) are also dangerous because they threaten to dispel

116

family myth, just as Uncle Nathan's revelation (" 'I
killed Mr. Dearman with a stone to his head, and let
'em hang a sawmill nigger for it,' " p. 344) shatters
the family myth of his goodness (" 'Now what did you
want to tell that for?' ", p. 344).

Ultimately, it is the power of language, the fear
that knowing oneself may destroy the self as well as
the belief that family grammar will rebuild the reunion
year after year, to which Losing Battles owes its
existence. In a sense, therefore, the journey is a
linguistic one that conjoins a family's historical and
mythical time frames in much the same way that
nationalism conjoins a nation's, or psychotherapy an
individual's. Because it is a journey back to the
eternal mythical present as well as forward in calendar
time, the journey to Banner completes circles in both
directions. The reunion celebrates the annual arrival
of family to its traditional center. It is an attempt,
as T. S. Eliot puts it, "... to arrive where we
started, / And know the place for the first time."[55]

[1] The most perceptive of the numerous studies treating the circle motif in Losing Battles is Michael Kreyling's "Myth and History: The Foes of Losing Battles" (Mississippi Quarterly, 26, Fall 1973), pp. 639-649.

[2] The constituent elements of the Southern Romance are the following: reference to classical mythology, regional mythology surrounding the Southern character, geographic legend and folktale, inter- and intra-family graphing, preoccupation with identity or name, acceptance of narrative authority, repetition of incident, and belief in the ability of language to order chaos.

[3] The term is borrowed from Robert Scholes and Robert Kellogg, The Nature of Narrative (London: Oxford University Press, 1966), p. 21.

[4] Eudora Welty, Losing Battles (New York: Random House, 1970), pp. 3-94.

[5] See E. V. Rieu's introduction to The Odyssey (Baltimore: Penguin Books, 1946), pp. 10-15.

[6] Carol A. Moore, in "The Insulation of Illusion and Losing Battles" (Mississippi Quarterly, 26, Fall 1973), pp. 650-658, defines the novel as displaying the "overtones" of "mock-epic comedy" (p. 657).

[7] An Anthology of Greek Drama. Ed. C. A. Robinson, Jr. (New York: Holt, Rinehart & Winston, 1949), p. vii.

[8] For the specific arrivals of Beecham-Vaughn-Renfro family members see pp. 8, 9, 71, 78, 188. Lady May has also "arrived" since Jack's departure for Parchman.

[9] See pp. 343, 356, 374-5 for the specific departures of the family members. The first reference to Miss Julia Mortimer's death occurs on p. 157. For the most concise statement of Grandpa Vaughn's death see p. 68. Both deaths are metaphorical departures in that they signal the end of representative cycles. Grandpa Vaughn's absence at the reunion marks a break

in the Vaughn-Beecham family circle, just as Miss Julia Mortimer's death marks the completion of her influence in Banner. As Judge Moody observes, " 'I suppose if I was the first of Miss Julia's protéges, this girl was her last' " (p. 325).

[10]Myths, Rites, and Symbols: A Mircea Eliade Reader. Ed. Wendell C. Beane and William G. Doty, Vol. I. (New York: Harper & Row, 1976), pp. 33-4.

[11]Although her study preceded publication of Losing Battles, Ruth M. Vande Kieft suggests, in Eudora Welty (New York: Twayne Publishers, Inc., 1962), that ritual action is highly important to Welty's art (p. 70).

[12]Mircea Eliade, Cosmos and History: The Myth of the Eternal Return (New York: Harper & Row, 1954), p. 17.

[13]As Thompson defines it, the märchen is "a tale of some length involving a succession of motifs or episodes. It moves in an unreal world without definite locality or definite characters and is filled with the marvelous." Stith Thompson, The Folktale (New York: The Dryden Press, 1951), p. 8.

[14]Throughout this study, I will be following J.R.R. Tolkien's distinction between "enchantment" and "magic" in his Tree and Leaf (Boston: Houghton Mifflin, 1965), pp. 52-3.

[15]See Northrop Frye, The Secular Scripture: A Study of the Structure of Romance (Cambridge: Harvard University Press, 1976), pp. 35-61.

[16]"Shangri-La South." Time (4 May 1970), p. 100.

[17]Thomas H. Landess, "More Trouble in Mississippi: Family vs. Antifamily in Miss Welty's Losing Battles." Sewanee Review, 79 (October-December 1971), p. 632.

[18]Michael Kreyling, "Myth and History: The Foes of Losing Battles," p. 640.

[19]As a symbol of continuous movement, the circle mimics life itself, and it is this kind of endless flux that sacred time seeks to fix, and that the

reunion is powerless against: "Brother Bethune's gun, still resting against the trunk, was travelling too, and nothing at all was unmovable, or empowered to hold the scene still fixed or stake the reunion there" (p. 223).

[20]William McMillen, "Circling-In: The Concept of Home in Eudora Welty's Losing Battles and The Optimist's Daughter." A Still Moment: Essays on the Art of Eudora Welty. Ed. John F. Desmond (London: The Scarecrow Press, Inc., 1978), p. 111.

[21]Lewis P. Simpson, "The Chosen People." Southern Review, 6 (July 1970), p. xix.

[22]For amplification of the parallels between the two women see "Everything Brought Out In The Open: Eudora Welty's Losing Battles," Louis D. Rubin, Jr. Hollins Critic, 7 (June 1970), p. 11. Rubin also treats parallels between the younger woman of the two works, Gloria Renfro and Virgie Rainey.

[23]See, for example, the comments of the aunts and uncles, pp. 234-236.

[24]John W. Aldridge, "Eudora Welty: Metamorphosis of a Southern Lady Writer." Saturday Review (11 April 1970), p. 36.

[25]Louise Y. Gossett, "Eudora Welty's New Novel: The Comedy of Loss." Southern Literary Journal, 3 (Fall 1970), p. 129.

[26]Michael Kreyling, "Myth and History: The Foes of Losing Battles," p. 644.

[27]R. D. Laing, The Politics of the Family (Massey Lectures, 8th Series. Toronto: The Hunter Rose Company, Publishers, 1969), pp. 10-11. Laing differentiates "projection" ("done by one person as his own experience, of the other") from "induction" ("done by one person to the other's experience") later in the essay (p. 46).

[28]Michael Kreyling notes this "reincarnation" in "Myth and History: The Foes of Losing Battles," p. 642.

[29]R. D. Laing, The Politics of the Family, p. 9.

[30]Eudora Welty, "The Radiance of Jane Austen." *The Eye of the Story* (New York: Random House, 1978), p. 7.

[31]The best thematic treatment of survival in *Losing Battles* is Lewis P. Simpson's "The Chosen People." *Southern Review*, 6 (July 1970, pp. xvii-xxiii.

[32]James Neault, in "Time in the Fiction of Eudora Welty" (*A Still Moment: Essays on the Art of Eudora Welty*), links Aunt Cleo with *Clio*, the Greek muse of history (p. 42). The identification is significant in that as successor to Granny Vaughn, Miss Beulah adopts the role of perpetuating the eternal mythical present through the rite of the reunion. She is therefore the natural enemy of Aunt Cleo, who is indeed the reunion's outsider, "from Southern Mississippi, Uncle Noah Webster's new wife" (p. 13).

[33]R. D. Laing, in *The Politics of the Family*, explains the term as the product of mapping: "You will be what I indicate you are" (pp. 12-13). Aunt Beck, for example, defines Gloria's role within the scenario (" 'that was her part,' " p. 93) as waiting.

[34]Jack's second arrival (after lodging Judge Moody's car on Banner Top for the night) is equally heroic (p. 189), and a mock-heroic identification is further strengthened when he refers to Banner at one point in the novel as "my realm" (p. 141).

[35]The primary value of the reunion is loyalty to the reunion itself. Miss Lexie abandons Miss Julia Mortimer because she "didn't want to fail the reunion" (p. 241), Aunt Nanny asks " 'what's wrong with a family any way you can get one?' " (p. 317), and Miss Lexie believes that the children would " 'like all life to be one grand reunion and never stop' " (p. 374).

[36]*Time* makes this observation in its review of *Losing Battles*, "Shangri-La South," (4 May 1970), p. 100.

[37]*Myths, Rites, and Symbols: A Mircea Eliade Reader*. Vol. 1 Ed. Wendell C. Beane, William G. Doty (New York: Harper & Row, 1976), pp. 152-3. Earlier in the text, Eliade has defined "hierophany" ("To designate the act of manifestation of the sacred, we have proposed the term hierophany," pp. 140-1) and "krato-

phany" (manifestation of power," p. 148). Eliade follows the above passage with L. Levy-Bruhl's comments on the composite nature of the "sacred" place: "... a sacred spot never presents itself to the mind in isolation. It is always part of a complexus of things which includes the plant or animal species which flourish there at various seasons, as well as the mythical heroes who lived, roamed or created something there and who are embodied in the very soil, the ceremonies which take place there from time to time, and all the emotions aroused by the whole" (p. 153).

[38]Eudora Welty, "Some Notes on River Country," The Eye of the Story, p. 286.

[39]The myth of Sam Dale Beecham is here reminiscent of that surrounding the portrait of Denis Fairchild in Delta Wedding, and his family mapping of George.

[40]Jonathan Yardley, in his review of Losing Battles, "The Last Good One?" (New Republic, 10 May 1970), sees the novel as the other side of Delta Wedding, with which it is locationally "symbiotic" (p. 35). For another comparison of the two works see Louise Y. Gossett, "Eudora Welty's New Novel: The Comedy of Loss," pp. 136-7.

[41]Although Gloria does have Jack by herself at one point in the novel ("Nobody talking, nobody listening, nobody coming -- nobody about to call you or walk in on us -- there's nobody left but you and me, and nothing to be in our way,' " p. 431), the isolation is temporary and the novel's ending ambiguous.

[42]Gloria's kinship through Rachel Sojourner to Aycock Comfort (p. 256) is similarly ironic in view of the animosity between the two over Jack (see pp. 111, 114).

[43]Eudora Welty, "Place in Fiction," The Eye of the Story, p. 128.

[44]Compare Gloria's statement " 'But you'll do it again,' she cried. 'Put me in the same fix! You risked your life for them!' " (pp. 421-2) with that of Robbie Reid after George Fairchild rescues his cousin Maureen from the Yazoo-Delta (p. 61). Neither is it insignificant that both women are referred to by their maiden names by the families they have married into.

[45]Michael Kreyling makes this association in "Myth and History: The Foes of Losing Battles," p. 647.

[46]Jan Harold Brunvand, The Study of American Folklore (New York: W. W. Norton & Company, Inc., 1968), p. 46. The text supports this association by attributing magical powers to Jack: " '... whatever he sticks in the ground, the Delta just grows it for him' " (p. 70).

[47]Michael Kreyling explores this relationship in "Myth and History: The Foes of Losing Battles," p. 641.

[48]The definition belongs to Robert Scholes and Robert Kellogg, The Nature of Narrative, p. 55.

[49]R. D. Laing, The Politics of the Family, p. 18.

[50]Andrew Lytle, "The Working Novelist and the Mythmaking Process." Myth and Mythmaking. Ed. Henry A. Murray (New York: George Braziller, Inc., 1960), p. 147.

[51]Edward Sapir. Language: An Introduction to the Study of Speech (New York: Harcourt, Brace, Jovanovich, 1921), 0. 38.

[52]Ibid., p. 90.

[53]As the references to tales and stories are far too numerous to quote here, the interested reader can find some of them on the following pages in the text: pp. 14, 17, 21-2, 32, 42, 49, 54, 55, 82, 113, 129, 137, 166, 177, 152, 196-7, 206-7, 214-5, 221, 272, 280, 335, 361, 372.

[54]References to these two forms can be found on the following pages of the text: the hymn, pp. 137-8, 227, 288, 436; the song, pp. 115, 128, 131, 223, 258, 269, 271, 307, 347-8, 407-8.

[55]T. S. Eliot, Four Quartets, The Complete Poems and Plays, 1909-1950 (Harcourt, Brace, & World, Inc., 1971), p. 145.

CHAPTER V. - THE OPTIMIST'S DAUGHTER

The most obvious difference between <u>The Opti-</u><u>mist's Daughter</u>[1] and Welty's earlier novels is its comparative silence. The narrative is neither, like <u>The Ponder Heart</u> and <u>Losing Battles</u>, a novel filled with colloquial voices, nor is it, like <u>The Robber</u> <u>Bridegroom</u> and <u>Delta Wedding</u>, permeated by the enchanted voice of the märchen. Rather, <u>The Optimist's</u>[2] <u>Daughter</u> is a novel preoccupied with vision; it is one that attempts "to see," not one that tries "to say." Like the aforementioned novels, however, <u>The Opti-</u><u>mist's Daughter</u> is a Southern Romance and its informing mythological pattern, like theirs, is the circle. Here, however, the circle not only traces a journey back into the past, but also inward, to a dark void of the self not unlike the one from which the reunion of <u>Losing Battles</u> had gathered to defend itself.

The narrative opens bluntly in the unnatural and antiseptic world of the modern hospital in which stark gesture has replaced lyric action.

> A nurse held the door open for them. Judge McKelva going first, then his daughter Laurel, then his wife Fay, they walked into the windowless room where the doctor would make his examination.[3]

In this opening passage, Judge, Laurel, and Fay McKelva follow one another into a darkened landscape that is where they remain, metaphorically at any rate, through most of the narrative. What vision is possible within this landscape is sporadic and arresting: objects are seen as with "the excruciatingly small, brilliant eye of the instrument" (p. 13) with which Dr. Courtland examines Judge McKelva's own eyesight. Images clearly envisioned, like the "watery constellation" that hangs "throbbing and near" outside Judge McKelva's window (p. 44), or Laurel's reflection in the train window looking to her like a beech tree "gliding along at a magic speed through the cypresses" (pp. 56-7), are doubly striking because viewed within a landscape which is itself "like a nowhere," "grayed-down, anonymous" (p. 23) -- a blindness.

The juxtaposition of blindness and insight echoes the Oedipal myth. In the myth, Tiresias, the blind prophet summoned by Oedipus to tell him his fate (that Oedipus is, paradoxically, the murderer he seeks), and Oedipus himself (whose act of self-blinding serves as a judgment on his lack of insight as well as an index of the level of self-knowledge he has attained) are both made wise in their blindness. The journey toward blindness and/or insight is cyclic; it moves both backward and forward in time. That is, Oedipus moves <u>forward</u> to a fate assigned to him in the <u>past</u>. He begins his journey in disbelief and metaphorical blindness and completes it in a literal blindness born of insight. The journey of <u>The Optimist's Daughter</u> is similarly constructed. Laurel's journey back into her past and the past of her parents (part 3, section 4; pp. 155-181) both leads her to an understanding of her father's relationship with her mother, and to the resurrection of her dead husband Phil.

> Now, by her own hands, the past had
> been raised up and <u>he</u> looked at
> her, Phil himself -- here waiting
> all the time, Lazarus. (p. 181)

Once she has arrived in the past Laurel is able to sleep, exhausted from the effort the night's work has cost her, "like a passenger who had come on an emergency journey in a train" (p. 185). Laurel's discovery of her mother's breadboard is a more precise example, for the moment of recovery -- the moment when her searching hands locate the breadboard Phil had made for her mother -- dovetails past and future in the form of Judge McKelva's wife Fay.

> In that same moment, she felt,
> more sharply than she could hear
> them where she was, footsteps that
> tracked through the parlor, the
> library, the hall, the dining
> room, up the stairs and through
> the bedrooms, down the stairs, in
> the same path Laurel had taken,
> and at last came to the kitchen
> door and stopped. (p. 199)

The cyclic journey that reaches both back and forward is symbolic of what Mircea Eliade would call "meaningful repetition."[4] For Judge McKelva, as for Clement

Musgrove in <u>The Robber Bridegroom</u>, however, the journey forward is the mirror image of the journey back.

Like Clement Musgrove, Judge McKelva has married twice, once "happily" (this marriage has produced a daughter) and once "unhappily" (Clement's second wife, Salome, is the ideal "wicked stepmother" of fairy tale, while Judge McKelva's, Wanda Fay, carries the fairy tale tradition in her name: wand, a dead stick; Fay, a spirit from underground.)[5] Guy Davenport's reading of the novel as a variation of the Persephone myth (Davenport sees Laurel as the living and Wanda Fay as the dead Persephone) and Cupid and Psyche myth (Phil, whose name literally is "love," forms the basis of this interpretation)[6] underscores the thematic separation of the novel into balanced halves, and reinforces the importance of the circle as its underlying myth symbol.

Like Clement, Judge McKelva is the center that holds antithetical poles (his two wives) in equilibrium. His position is demonstrated at the funeral, by attendants who "slowly moved in place, as if they made up the rim of a wheel that slowly turned itself around the hub of the coffin and would bring them around again" (p. 79). Laurel's primary objection to Fay's marriage with her father is significant in terms of this mythic configuration, for Fay has invaded the family circle and thus disturbed the "zone of absolute reality":[7] "You desecrated this house" (p. 200). Identified early in the narrative as a designer (p. 25), Laurel sees this configuration because she has been trained to look for patterns. She perceives her routine at the hospital as a pattern (p. 26), her memory of "firelight and warmth" (p. 158) owes much to "patterns, families, on the sweet-smelling matting, with the shine of firelight, or the summer light, moving over mother and child and what they both were making" (p. 159), and she recalls that Phil "taught her to draw, to work toward and into her pattern, not to sketch peripheries" (p. 188). In a sense, therefore, the novel is Laurel's attempt to see a pattern in apparent chaos, to find a way out of the Labyrinth whose Minotaur is blindness.

> Laurel had never noticed the tiling before, like some clue she would need to follow to get to the right place. But of course the last door on the right of the corridor, the one standing partway

open as usual, was still her
father's. (pp. 42-3)

In a sense, Laurel's completion of the journey, her
ability to see a pattern, insures the novel's comic
resolution. For, as Reynolds Price puts it in "The
Onlooker, Smiling: An Early Reading of The Optimist's
Daughter," "all patterns are comic ... because the universe is patterned, therefore ordered₈ and ruled, therefore incapable of ultimate tragedy."[8]

The circular journey of The Optimist's Daughter
leads, as we have said, both back and forward in time
and is, at least partially, a journey toward knowledge
and redemption. To complete her journey, Laurel, like
Oedipus, must come to terms with parental ghosts.
Throughout the novel, Laurel's mother Becky recurs to
counterpoint the Judge's wife Fay. First recalled in
conjunction with the McKelva fig tree (p. 11), Becky's
presence increases with her husband's blindness,
reminding both Laurel (p. 16) and Dr. Courtland (p.
15) that she suffered a similar blindness before her
death. Fay is first to observe Becky's presence
(" 'Why he hadn't even mentioned Becky, till you and
Courtland started him,' " p. 26), and even refers to
"Becky" although she "never called anyone by name" (p.
36). The chorus of neighbor ladies that visits Laurel
(in part 3, chapter 1) is still remembered as "Becky's
Garden Club" (p. 66), and Judge McKelva's funeral is,
in some ways, the completion of Becky's: " 'Do you
know, Laurel, who was coming to my mind the whole
blessed way through? Becky!' " (p. 121). Associated
with plants and flowers throughout the novel, at one
point Becky literally speaks to her daughter as Laurel
gardens: "Her mother's voice came back with each weed
she reached for, and its name with it. 'Ironweed.'
'Just chickweed.' 'Here comes that miserable old
vine!' " (p. 127).

Becky's ghost is evoked most completely, however,
by the secretary "made of the cherry trees on the
McKelva place a long time ago" (p. 159). The secretary, housing twenty-six compartments in which "her
mother had stored things according to their time and
place" (p. 160), is not only the means through which
Becky is brought into the present, but also the vehicle
that takes Laurel into the past. Not insignificantly,
it is locating the photograph album that, appropriately
enough, brings time and place into focus.

> Still clinging to the first
> facing pages were the pair of
> grayed and strippled home-printed
> snapshots: Clinton and Becky "up
> home", each taken by the other
> standing in the same spot on a
> railroad track (a leafy glade), he
> slender as a wand, his foot on a
> milepost, swinging his straw hat;
> she with her hands full of the
> wildflowers they'd picked along
> the way. (pp. 161-2)

Railroad track and flowers are as symptomatic of
Laurel's mother as are library books and papers of her
father, and the sections treating Laurel's exploration
of these places (pp. 159-180; pp. 139-145) form com-
panion pieces that both bring her parents to her, and
complete her own journey cycle. For Laurel is only
able to leave Mount Salus after her parents' ghosts
have been laid to rest. The journey redeems memory
with suffering and is therefore heroic.

> Memory lived not in initial pos-
> session but in the freed hands,
> pardoned and freed, and in the
> heart that can empty but fill
> again, in the patterns restored by
> dreams. (pp. 207-8)

Like Oedipus, Laurel chooses knowledge though it brings
her pain. As John A. Allen explains the act of heroism
in his discussion of Virgie Rainey and The Golden
Apples, "her heroism does not derive from what is
usually thought of as heroic action but from her capacity to feel and, through feeling, to know."[9] The heroic
act is thus the accomplishment of insight that allows
Laurel to slay the Minotaur and escape the Labyrinth.

In The Optimist's Daughter, the labyrinth partakes of regional as well as classical myth. Blindness
keeps Becky away from her West Virginia mountains long
after fire has destroyed her reason to go (p. 76)
because "up home" is a symbolic location --a place
blindness and illness have kept her from. Instead of
returning home, Becky dies believing that "she had been
taken somewhere that was neither home nor 'up home',
that she was left among strangers. ... she had died
without speaking a word, keeping everything to herself,
in exile and humiliation" (p. 177). Laurel's marriage

("of magical ease, of _ease_ -- of brevity and conclusion and all belonging to Chicago and not here," p. 143), like her mother's youth, has been sealed within region where it has become mythic in its inviolability. For both Becky and her daughter, region lends significance to event. Certain insights (like the perfection of Laurel's marriage) only occur within the rare conjunction of the right place and time. The relationship is made explicit by Becky to the Presbyterian preacher, Dr. Bolt, in relation to the wild strawberries she had seen when young.

> 'And on that mountain, young man, there's a white strawberry that grows completely in the wild, if you know where to look for it. I think it very likely grows in only one spot in the world. I could tell you this minute where to go, but I doubt if you'd see them growing after you got there. Deep in the woods, you'd miss them. You could find them by mistake, and you could line your hat with leaves and try to walk off with a hatful: that would be how little you knew abut those berries. Once you've let them so much as touch each other, you've already done enough to finish 'em.' She fixed him with her nearly sightless eyes. 'Nothing you ever ate in your life was anything like as delicate, as fragrant, as those wild white strawberries. You had to know enough to go where they are and stand and eat them on the spot, that's all.' (p. 175)

In order not to miss what time and place offer only rarely, one must stand still and experience the mystery of place. Like the wild white strawberries, significance adheres to region. Recalled, the mystery of place becomes regional myth.

Sections of Mississippi, Texas, and Virginia are as symbolic as Becky's West Virginia mountains, and form regional indexes of character. In his "The Onlooker, Smiling: An Early Reading of The Optimist's Daughter," Reynolds Price explains the significance of

location in terms of class: "Virginians are finer than
Mississippians are finer than Texans."[10] Judge McKelva
who, "like his father had attended the University of
Virginia" (p. 162) is, in fact, one of the social and
political leaders of the Mount Salus community. His
appropriate mate is Becky, for even though she is from
West Virginia, her parents are both Virginians and her
father is a lawyer (p. 163). The next highest level of
regional significance, the level directly below the
Virginians in terms of status, is the Mount Salus community itself. It is on this level that Dr. Courtland,
himself a native of Mississippi, addresses Laurel in
New Orleans the night of her father's death:
" 'Laurel, there's nobody from home with you. Would
you care to put up with us for the rest of the
night?' " (p. 53). After her father's death, Laurel's
family, her "people," are the members of the community
in which she was raised. It is because her Mount Salus
friends are communal "kin" that Laurel is reprimanded
by her mother's friends for the double betrayal of
leaving her father (" 'Yes, daughters need to stay put,
where they can keep a better eye on us old folks,' " p.
76) and marrying a Northerner (" 'She didn't look at
home to find Philip Hand,' " p. 137): " 'Laurel is who
should have saved him from that nonsense. Laurel
shouldn't have married a naval officer in wartime.
Laurel should have stayed home after Becky died' " (p.
136). It is because Laurel is a Mississippian that she
is discouraged from returning to Chicago.

> 'Once you leave after this,
> you'll always come back as a visi-
> tor,' Mrs. Pease warned Laurel.
> 'Feel free, of course -- but
> it was always my opinion that peo-
> ple don't really want visitors.'
> (p. 133)

Among other reasons, Mrs. Pease and the chorus of
Becky's friends want Laurel to "stay put" so she can
protect the Judge's house from Wanda Fay McKelva. Even
though she is obviously lowest in the novel's social
hierarchy, Fay is proud of her region and refuses to be
mistaken for a Mississippian: " 'I'm not from Mississippi. I'm from Texas.' She let out a long cry" (p.
48). Described by Guy Davenport as one of the "rapa-
cious, weak-witted, pathologically selfish daughters
of the dispossessed,"[11] Fay is reduced to, and
explained away by, "her origins" (p. 126). In thus
categorizing Fay, the chorus of Becky's friends is

making a statement about the interdependence of family and place. Fay's pride in her origins is therefore a comment on her character, a way of indexing her by region.

Within the region around Mount Salus, Judge McKelva is a local legend nearly as strong as Miss Julia Mortimer is in the uphill Mississippi region within which Losing Battles takes place. Like her, Judge McKelva is celebrated the day of his funeral by a community to which he largely remains a mystery. Even though his friends arrive to pay their respects to his body (" '. . . your father's a Mount Salus man. He's a McKelva. A public figure. You can't deprive the public, can you?' " p. 78), they have forgotten what his life has signified (" 'They're trying to say for a man that his life is over. Do you know a good way?' " p. 100). As those of Miss Julia Mortimer's, the details of Judge McKelva's life are unimportant. What is significant is the power of his legend.

> Laurel saw that there had not been room enough in the church for everybody who had come. All around the walls, people were standing; they darkened the colored glass of the windows. Black Mount Salus had come too, and the black had dressed themselves in black. (p. 107)

Although Becky is remembered by her friends and daughter, Judge McKelva is honored by a community for which his funeral is, as Cleanth Brooks notes, "in the most profound sense a social occasion."[12]

In The Optimist's Daughter, the occasion of Judge McKelva's illness and death provides the framework within which family myth operates. The "social occasion" here provides what Welty has elsewhere called the "narrative sense" of a family: "a sense of what happened to them and probably why, because look what happened to her grandmother."[13] Family myth is thus intergenerational. The McKelva family (Judge, Becky, and Laurel) is set against other families central to the novel (Dalzells and Chisoms) through the experience of loss. Unlike her other novels, The Optimist's Daughter is a portrait of the way in which three sets of estranged family members interact when brought together during the occasion of illness and death. For

132

the McKelvas, estrangement consists of Laurel's removal to Chicago, her mother's death, and her father's remarriage. In a sense, the Judge's illness is symptomatic of estrangement and his death allows for Laurel's discovery of family myth. Initially, Judge McKelva's illness is made familial in his choice of Dr. Courtland as physician. It is because Dr. Courtland is from Mount Salus, had treated Becky during her illness, and is close to the family, that Judge McKelva chooses him to perform the operation on his eye: " 'I'm in good hands, Fay,' Judge McKelva told her. 'I know his whole family' " (p. 18). Ironically, however, precisely what Judge McKelva perceives as reasons to proceed with the operation hold Dr. Courtland against performing it.

> 'Laurel,' he said, 'I don't
> want to do this operation myself.'
> He went on quickly, 'I've kept
> being so sorry about your mother.'
> He turned and gave what might have
> been his first direct look at Fay.
> 'My family's known his family for
> such a long time...' (p. 15)

The comments of the two men provide a context of family (McKelva) within family (Mount Salus community) that is sustained throughout the novel. Within this context, family myth is twofold, encompassing not only Mount Salus's perception of the McKelvas, but also Laurel's perceptions of her father, her mother, and Fay.

At the funeral, guests from the larger family ("the County Bar, the elders of the church, the Hunting and Fishing Club cronies," p. 79)[1] testify to Judge McKelva's bravery (p. 97), theatrical flair (p. 98), and sense of humor (p. 99), even though Laurel insists to Miss Adele that they are "misrepresenting him -- falsifying" (p. 101). At his death, Judge McKelva has been translated from family member (in this larger sense) to family myth. Because the translation is communal, it is the medium through which Judge McKelva becomes a kind of family hero. His alleged theatrical talent, for example, is clearly seen by Laurel as Major Bullock's addition to the heroic myth (" 'He's trying to make Father into something he wanted to be himself,' " p. 98), while "the work he had done on floods and flood control" (p. 141) is either forgotten by his celebrants or edited from his communal definition as representative of unheroic "drudgery" (p. 142). The

133

communal perceptions of Judge McKelva thus form a type
of family myth that, although at odds with the facts of
his life, gains strength from his status as a local
legend.

Although Laurel is disturbed by the community's
misrepresentation of her father, she is as guilty of
misperceiving his personal life as is the community of
mythologizing his public life. Early in the novel,
Laurel notices Judge McKelva's "delicacy" to "family
feelings" (p. 28). This delicacy is initially conjoined with an overriding optimism, a belief that all
will turn out well in the end whether in his communal
(" 'There was never anything wrong with keeping up a
little optimism over the Flood,' " p. 143) or personal
life ("'Well, I'm an optimist,' " p. 17). Gradually,
however, Judge McKelva's optimism seems, to Laurel, to
waver: "He, who had been the declared optimist, had
not once expressed hope. Now it was she who was offering it
to him" (p. 39). It is only late in the novel that Laurel
perceives her father's optimism for what it has been all
along, a defense against his "delicacy."

> He grimaced with delicacy. What he
> could not control was his belief that
> all his wife's troubles would turn out
> all right because there was nothing he
> would not have given her. (p. 172)

The private myth thus feeds the communal, which is in turn
translated into heroism. Because Judge McKelva cannot
alleviate his wife's suffering, his books become a "family" (p.
140) initially shared by them both, but increasingly a shelter
from the pain of loss.

> When he reached a loss he simply put
> on his hat and went speechless out of
> the house to his office and worked for
> an hour or so getting up a brief for
> somebody. (p. 72)

Ironically, however, the briefs are themselves mis-
remembered communally, so that Judge McKelva's optimism
is symptomatic of a perceptual failure, an inability to see his
wife's illness in perspective.

> ... he might have dredged the word up
> out of his childhood. He loved

his wife. Whatever she did that
she couldn't help doing was all
right. Whatever she was driven to
say was all right. But it was not
all right! Her trouble was that
very desperation. And no one had
the power to cause that except the
one she desperately loved, who
refused to consider that she was
desperate. (p. 176)

It is therefore not insignificant that Judge McKelva's
death is associated with a failure of insight of which
faulty eyesight is symptomatic: "Judge McKelva had
recalled himself at Becky's Climber" (p. 135). Once
his eyes are bandaged ("He never asked about his eye.
He never mentioned his eye," p. 27), Judge McKelva
begins the journey within, of waiting "full of effort
yet motionless" (p. 31), that ends in death: " 'He's
gone, and his eye was healing' " (p. 52).

With her family's death, Laurel begins to unravel
the family myth that had surrounded her youth. The
novel's movement is, in fact, Laurel's movement away
from her initial belief that " 'some things don't bear
going into' " (p. 53). Laurel's journey begins with
her father's operation and progresses back to childhood, helplessness, and confusion. After awakening
from surgery, Judge McKelva signals the transition into
the past not only by referring to Laurel as "Polly" but
also by recalling Becky as if she were in the room with
them.

'What's the verdict?' her
father presently asked, in a
parched voice. 'Eh, Polly?' He
called Laurel by her childhood
name. 'What's your mother have to
say about me?' (p. 24)

Laurel's futile attempt to awaken Judge McKelva from
his "dream of patience" (p. 33) in the hospital proves
as futile as Mr. Dalzell's attempt to convince his
hearers that the judge is "his long-lost son Archie
Lee" (p. 30). The juxtaposition of the two points of
view is ironic in that however different, both fail
equally to penetrate Judge McKelva's isolated self. In
other words, Judge McKelva is as remote to Laurel as is
Mr. Dalzell to his estranged son. Laurel is as incapable of saving her father as is Mr. Dalzell of recog-

nizing his son. In a sense, therefore, Judge McKelva dies believing, as did his wife Becky, that he is among strangers. The myth of family cohesion and comfort thus fails for Laurel as it had for her father at his wife's death (p. 177), and for Becky at the death of her father (p. 169). As Laurel puts it late in the novel, " 'we were a family of comparatively helpless people -- that's what so bound us, bound us together' " (p. 203).

If helplessness supplants comfort, then so does ambivalence supplant certainty. One of Laurel's realizations at her father's funeral is that she can never really know Judge McKelva. The way in which the community had mythologized her father as a public figure thus merely accentuates Laurel's own perpetuation of family myth in refusing to relinquish the past. Laurel's mistake is in denying the complexity of the past and in equating past and present. Prior to her return to Mount Salus, Laurel had understood her parents' marriage as one of complete harmony, one like her own. She had been certain that her father's love for her mother, like her love for Phil, could not harm Becky. With her father's death, the years of Laurel's estrangement from him are brought home to her in the form of Fay. She is forced to examine the present, which in turn leads her to reexamine the past. If the present mystifies her, then so must the past since the present is determined by it. Her very certainty is her ignorance, for it precludes her from seeing ambivalence and ambiguity. As she realizes at one point in the novel, "the mystery in how little we know of other people is no greater than the mystery of how much" (p. 99). Once she admits to uncertainty, Laurel can begin to understand the myth she has created.

The myth surrounding Judge McKelva's marriage to Becky is exposed to Laurel in the reality of his marriage to Fay. As we have said, Fay is the mirror image of Becky. Concerned with outward appearances (" 'I'm glad you can't see yourself, hon,' " p. 25; " 'Look! Look what I got to match my eardrops! How do you like 'em, hon? Don't you want to let's go dancing?' "p. 37), Fay is as frightened by the darkness of Dr. Courtland's office as a child, and feels herself powerless within it: " 'It's dark!' Fay gave a little cry. 'Why did he have to go back there anyway and get mixed up in those brambles?' " (p. 12). Failing to understand her husband's illness, Fay insists that the best cure is no cure at all (" 'Why not leave it to Nature?' Fay said.

'That's what I keep on telling him,' " p. 13;
" 'Nature's the great healer,' " p. 17). Her concerns
in New Orleans are consistently those of the child
failing to get her way.

> 'What a way to keep his pro-
> mise,' said Fay. 'When he told me
> he'd bring me to New Orleans some
> day, it was to see the Carnival.'
> She stared out the window. 'And
> the Carnival's on right now. It
> looks like this is as close as
> we'll get to a parade.' (p. 21)

Throughout the novel, Fay's preoccupation is Fay herself. In this self-centered envelope Fay is a
malicious version of <u>Delta Wedding</u>'s Robbie Reid and
<u>Losing Battles</u>'s Gloria Short. Like them, Fay denies
history (" 'The past isn't a thing to me. I belong to
the future, didn't you know that?' " p. 207.) Her sense
of self is based on where she finds herself and what
she sees in relation to herself (" 'Why did I have to
be shown that?' "; " 'Nobody told me <u>this</u> was going to
happen to me!' " p. 15), and her sense of relationship
is rather a form of presentation: " 'Look-a-here!'
exclaimed Fay. She jumped up and pattered toward his
bed in her stockinged feet. 'Who's <u>this</u>?' She pointed
to the gold button over her breastbone" (p. 24).
Suspicious of family relationships which are based on
history and the past (such as Judge McKelva's relationship with Dr. Courtland, pp. 18, 19, 54), Fay goes so
far as to deny her own family out of existence (" 'My
family?' said Fay, 'none of 'em living,' " p. 37).

> 'You said you had nobody --no
> family.   You lied about your
> family.'
> 'If I did, that's what every-
> body else does,' said Fay. 'Why
> shouldn't I?' (p. 119)

The lie is a perversion of the mythmaking process. It
is denial rather than misperception, destruction
rather than creation. As John A. Allen observes, Fay
is "ideally ill-equipped for genuine heroic action"
because she is "deficient both in feeling and in sense
of reality, and therefore all but incapable of love."[15]

Rather than holding the memory of home after it
has been destroyed, as does Becky, Fay obliterates

memory to sustain a myth of homelessness and pastless-
ness. Belonging entirely to the moment, Fay believes
in action over talk and talk over books. In her judgment, her husband's failing eyesight is a product of
too much reading: " 'I told him if he hadn't spent so
many years of his life poring over dusty old books, his
eyes would have more strength saved for now' "(p. 35).
Fay's spontaneity is mirrored by Becky's patience.
Associated throughout the novel with flowers, Becky
shares the gardener's secret of knowing how to wait:
"If it didn't bloom this year, it would next: 'That's
how gardeners must learn to look at it,' her mother
would say" (pp. 135-6). Although they are intrin-
sically opposite, Fay and Becky are not rivals, as
Laurel comes to realize late in the novel.

> It's not between the living and
> the dead, between the old wife and
> the new; it's between too much
> love and too little. There is no
> rivalry as bitter; Laurel had seen
> its work. (p. 178)

In a sense, therefore, Fay completes Becky by providing
her counterpart. The rivalry between them exists
within Judge McKelva himself. With this understanding,
Laurel can accept the possibility of Fay's existence
within her family: " 'Fay, my mother knew you'd get in
her house. She never needed to be told,' said Laurel.
'She predicted you' " (p. 201).

With the appearance of the Dalzells, Laurel's
sense of what it means to belong to a family is
expanded, and with the Chisoms it is refined. As in
Welty's other novels, the circle is here symbolic of
family unity and cohesion. The earliest description of
the Dalzell family notes a circular configuration ("the
circle pulled up around a table... a family in the
middle of their supper," p. 47) that is reinforced
several pages later by the family's tendency to respond
"almost in a chorus" (p. 49) of laughter or speech (pp.
50-1). Watching the Dalzells who, despite their lack
of sophistication are indeed a family, prepares Laurel
for the intrusion of the Chisoms at her father's funeral. Invited by Major Bullock (p. 85), the Chisoms
complete the family portrait begun in the hospital by
the Dalzells.[16] When she first meets them, Laurel
feels "that she had seen them all before" (p. 85).
Like the Dalzells, Fay's family shares a sense of
cohesion and unity against outsiders (" 'Friends are

here today and gone tomorrow,' Mrs. Chisom told Laurel and the Mayor. 'Not like your kin,' " p. 86) -- a disclosure that is literal as well as figurative.

> 'Yes, me and my brood believes in clustering just as close as we can get,' said Mrs. Chisom. 'Bubba pulled his trailer right up in my yard when he married and Irma can string her clothesline as far out as she pleases. Sis here got married and didn't even try to move away. Duffy just snuggled in.' (p. 87)

To Laurel, Dalzells and Chisoms both belong to "the great, interrelated family of those who never know the meaning of what has happened to them" (p. 103). Once she has made this connection, Laurel is better able to perceive Fay.

As in Losing Battles, the cohesive family here maintains and perpetuates itself through what R. D. Laing defines as a process of "mapping."[17] Laurel observes how Fay's nephew Wendell is being prepared by Mrs. Chisom, through this process of mapping, to fill Roscoe's position in their family.

> "He went down fast and we buried him back in Mississippi, back in Bigbee, and there on the spot I called Roscoe to me." She pulled Wendell to her now. " 'Roscoe,' I says, 'you're the mainstay now,' I says, 'you're the head of the Chisom family.' He was so happy." Wendell began to cry. (p. 94)

Through Wendell's innocence, Laurel comes to acknowledge the possibility of Fay's ("So Fay might have appeared, just at the beginning, to her aging father, with his slipping eyesight," p. 94). What happened to Fay, and what will inevitably happen to Wendell, is submission to the family pattern. If Mrs. Chisom can map herself onto Fay, as her behavior at Judge McKelva's funeral suggests (" 'Like mother, like daughter. Though when I had to give up her dad, they couldn't hold me half so easy. I tore up the whole house, I did,' " p. 104), then she is sure to map

139

Roscoe onto Wendell as well. Watching the creation of a family's mythology helps Laurel to better perceive what it means to belong to a family.

As in Welty's other novels, most notably The Ponder Heart and Losing Battles, behavioral standards are here supplied by narrative point of view. According to Laurel, Fay's flaw, and the flaw of the Chisoms as a family, is failing to perceive significance. After a lengthy discussion (pp. 125-132), the chorus of Becky's friends decides that Fay's behavior is neither better nor worse than that of her family (" 'I gathered from the evidence we were given that Fay was emulating her own mother' "; " 'We can't find fault with doing that, can we, Laurel?' " p. 132). Throughout the discussion, Laurel comments neither on Fay's behavior nor on that of the communal family during Judge McKelva's funeral. Her silence is important, however, in accentuating Laurel's separateness and refusal not only to judge Fay, but also to judge her mother's friends. The narrative point of view is made Laurel's, but only by implication. It is a visual point of view, the point of view of an outsider watching what is being revealed. By aligning the reader's vision with that of what Reynolds Price has called the "onlooker,"[18] Welty insures the acceptance of narrator (or rather presiding consciousness) as authority. When Laurel witnesses her father's death, for example, the scene is rendered objectively, yet through Laurel's point of view.

> The door stood wide open, and inside the room's darkness a watery constellation hung, throbbing and near. She was looking straight out at the whole Mississippi River Bridge in lights. She found her way, the night light was burning. Her father's right arm was free of the cover and lay out on the bed. It was bare to the shoulder, its skin soft and gathered, like a woman's sleeve. It showed her that he was no longer concentrating. (p. 44)

Images of bridge and arm are first presented objectively and then located within Laurel's point of view. Thus, the "watery constellation" reflects back to Laurel ("she was looking straight out at the whole Mis-

sissippi River Bridge in lights"), just as the "soft
and gathered" skin of her father leads to an insight
("It showed her that he was no longer concentrating").
Passages like these concretize the novel's narrative
focus and prepare the reader to accept the journey into
night that closes Book 3 (chapter 4, pp. 155-181).

It is not surprising, therefore, that the primary
event with which this journey is preoccupied is visual
rather than narrative. The event Laurel remembers is
one of "confluence."

> When they were climbing the
> long approach to a bridge after
> leaving Cairo, rising slowly
> higher until they rode above the
> tops of bare trees, she looked
> down and saw the pale light
> widening and the river bottoms
> opening out, and then the water
> appearing, reflecting the low,
> early sun. There were two rivers.
> Here was where they came together.
> This was the confluence of the
> waters, the Ohio and the Missis-
> sippi.
> They were looking down from a
> great elevation and all they saw
> was at the point of coming togeth-
> er, the bare trees marching in
> from the horizon, the rivers
> moving into one, and as he touched
> her arm she looked up with him and
> saw the long, ragged, pencil-faint
> line of birds within the crystal
> of the zenith, flying in a V of
> their own, following the same
> course down. All they could see
> was sky, water, birds, light, and
> confluence. It was the whole
> morning world.
> And they themselves were a
> part of the confluence. Their own
> joint act of faith matched its
> occurrence, and proceeded as it
> proceeded. Direction itself was
> made beautiful, momentous. They
> were riding as one with it, right
> up front. It's our turn! she'd

141

thought exultantly. And we're
going to live forever. (p. 186)

For Laurel, confluence is the perfect moment on a
space-time grid made complete through the act of perception. The significance of this episode therefore
lies within the relationship between scene and per-
ceiver. Like the speaker in Wallace Stevens's "The
Snow Man," the observer here becomes part of the scene
as it is described, and participation leads the
observer to insight, a creation of the eye rather than
the mind. In One Time, One Place, Welty makes this
relationship explicit.

> If exposure is essential, still
> more so is the reflection.
> Insight doesn't happen often on
> the click of the moment, like a
> lucky snapshot, but comes in its
> own time and more slowly and from
> nowhere but within. (p. 354)

Laurel's understanding of confluence, like her
mother's understanding of the wild strawberries, is
reflection made significant through insight. In a
sense, the novel is itself a confluence not only for
Judge McKelva, moving between two wives simulta-
neously, "holding onto them both, then letting them go"
(p. 198), but also for Laurel. It is the record of a
convergence, an acceptance of separateness which
Laurel recognizes as "the truth of the heart" (pp. 201-
2).

Laurel's progress toward an acceptance of
ambiguity, or double-vision if you will, takes her from
comparing past and present (the way her room looked in
the past and looks when she returns, pp. 70-1; the
changes in her mother's room, p. 75; the graveyard at
her father's funeral, pp. 108-11) to superimposing past
and present, perceiving each as separate yet conjoined.
The moment of transition is perfectly illustrated in
Laurel's argument with Fay over the breadboard Phil had
made for her mother. Once "sound and beautiful" (p.
204), the breadboard has been abused by Fay, who
cracked last year's walnuts on it (p. 200). Laurel's
initial reaction, to take the breadboard back to
Chicago and work at restoring it (p. 204), is modified
by the realization that "the whole story ... the whole
solid past" (p. 206) that it represents is as imper
vious to Fay's harm as it is to her own help.

Confluence, the joining of opposites, is as inevitable in the symbol of the breadboard as in that of her husband's death.

> For there is hate as well as love, she supposed, in the coming together and continuing of our lives. She thought of Phil and the kamikaze shaking hands. (p. 205)

Love and hate dovetail in the image of Phil's death, just as past and present coexist in the image of the breadboard. What Laurel learns through confluence is to see each separately yet superimposed, the grief of the bridesmaids through their laughter.

Confluence plays tricks with time. During her train ride to Mount Salus, for example, the passage of time is signalled to Laurel, as to the reader, through the cinematic technique of the dissolve.

> As the train left the black swamp and pulled out into the space of Ponchartrain, the window filled with a featureless sky over pale smooth water, where a seagull was hanging with wings fixed, like a stopped clock on a wall. She must have slept, for nothing seemed to have changed before her eyes until the seagull became the hands on the clock in the Courthouse dome lit up in the night above Mount Salus trees. (p. 57)

The seagull dissolves into its metaphorical counterpart, the image of a fixed clock. Connected here, time, like vision, predominates the novel. After its initial haste (the hurry to operate on Judge McKelva that dominates its early pages, p. 14), the novel slows to a point at which past and future become confused. The novel's preoccupation with time becomes obtrusive during Judge McKelva's "recovery" period, when his eye requires that he remain stationary and wait (pp. 24, 27, 31). This early preoccupation is expressed both in Dr. Courtland's satisfaction that Laurel can take the time to remain with her father (p. 5) and in the request of Judge McKelva, newly returned from surgery, of the time (pp. 25-6). This early

concen tration upon time gradually
shifts to a pacing in which Laurel
slows to her father's sense of
time,

... she was conscious of time
along with him, setting her inner
chronology with his, more or less
as if they needed to keep in step
for a long walk ahead of them.
(pp. 28-9)

while Judge McKelva in turn marks hers.

... Judge McKelva, holding himself
motionless, listened to her read,
then turn the page, as if he were
silently counting, and knew each
page by its number. (p. 29)[19]

The pace established by Laurel and her father is at
odds with that of the hospital and its representative,
Dr. Courtland. Up until Judge McKelva's death, Dr.
Courtland measures the progress of his eye's recovery
by the clock. When trying to save his life, Dr.
Courtland realizes (as he had realized early in the
novel) that there is "no time to lose" (p. 46), and it
is not insignificant that he appears in the doorway
after the attempt has failed with "the weight of his
watch in his hand" (p. 52). For Laurel, death comes to
signal a reversal of the direction in which time moves.
The living, of whom Dr. Courtland is symbolic in his
role of healer, push time forward, while the dying
regress back into time: "When he could no longer get
up and encourage it, push it forward, had it turned on
him, started moving back the other way?" (p. 178).
Judge McKelva's "unnatural reticence" (p. 32) is therefore ironic. The "obedience of an old man" (p. 31)
that Laurel sees within her father is ultimately not
obedience to the hospital staff, but rather submission
to the reversal of time. It is a gesture signalling
the loss of an ability to control duration.

With her father's death, Laurel's understanding
of time sharpens. The drive back to the Hibiscus,
during which "Laurel was still gearing herself to the
time things took" (p. 54), becomes an opportunity for
insight into Fay's character.

144

'I saw a man -- I saw a man and he was dressed up like a skeleton and his date was in a long white dress, with snakes for hair, holding up a bunch of lilies! Coming down the steps of that house like they're just coming out!' Then she cried out again, the longing, or the anger, of her whole life all in her voice at one time, 'Is it the Carnival?' (p. 55)

Removed by her father's death from what is taking place around her, Laurel is better able to perceive the revelation presented to her. As Welty puts it in One Time, One Place, "the thing to wait on, to reach there in time for, is the moment in which people reveal[20] themselves. You have to be ready, in yourself." Once ready, Laurel is able to return to Mount Salus, where the polarity between herself and Fay is further emphasized through time and its symbol, the timepiece. Prior to the funeral, for example, Laurel notices that the mantel clock has stopped, not having been wound since her father left for the hospital. The clock is eventually wound by one of the bridesmaids (p. 113), and its ticking, or, more precisely, the reminder of the hour, upsets Fay for whom the past is non-existent.

The clock struck for half-past twelve.
'Oh, how I hate that old striking clock!' cried Fay. 'It's the first thing I'm going to get rid of.' (p. 120)

Ironically, Laurel learns a great deal about the past from Fay. In a sense, Fay is pastless because, as Laurel realizes, "Fay could have walked in early as well as late, she could have come at any time at all. She was coming" (p. 202). Like the two rivers Laurel remembers, Becky and Fay move toward the moment of confluence, each from a different direction. There is no past and future, because the existence of one presupposes the existence of the other: they must arrive together, "in some convulsion of the mind" (p. 201).

It is this understanding of confluence that allows Laurel to perceive betrayal as a condition that transcends time. Although she does not appear until after Becky's death, Fay is Becky's betrayal.

145

> Her mother had suffered in life
> every symptom of having been
> betrayed, and it was not until she
> had died, and the protests of
> memory came due, that Fay had ever
> tripped in from Madrid, Texas.
> (p. 201)

Fay therefore completes a betrayal begun with Judge
McKelva's optimism. The paradox of causing the one
closest the greatest pain is the "betrayal on betrayal"
(p. 176) that the inevitability of Fay concludes. If
death is betrayal (p. 178), then so is outliving the
one who has died (p. 189). Perceiving this paradox is
understanding the "heroic act" of Perseus as John A.
Allen defines it in "Eudora Welty: The Three Moments."

> In the first moment of the heroic
> stroke, the hero wields the sword;
> in the second moment, he becomes
> the victim of that stroke. In the
> third moment, he achieves some
> measure of gain in understanding
> which leads on to self-renewal.[21]

As we have said, Laurel's journey is one of discovery
and redemption. For Laurel, self-renewal is accom-
plished through learning to see the past in a broader
perspective -- i.e., learning to accept the paradox
that hero and victim are one and the same.

Coming to terms with event entails coming to terms
with memory. Judge McKelva explains the cause of his
injury as a failure of memory (" 'Of course, my memory
had slipped ... before blooming is the wrong time to
prune a climber,' " p. 121), and Laurel laments the
community's failure to correctly remember her father at
his funeral (pp. 41-2). Her trip to Mount Salus
teaches Laurel to recognize the unpredictability of
memory and its power over time.

> Memory returned like spring,
> Laurel thought. Memory had the
> character of spring. In some
> cases it was the old wood that did
> the blooming. (p. 136)

Laurel is initially concerned with preserving memory
objectively in preserving her parents' belongings as
she knew them in her youth. Once she realizes that Fay

has altered the past, however, Laurel begins to erase it by erasing Fay (the drops of nail polish carelessly spilled by Fay on her father's desk, p. 145), and by burning "her father's letters to her mother, and Grandma's letters and the saved little books and papers" (p. 196) belonging to her parents. Once the house has been stripped of event ("There was nothing she was leaving in the whole shining and quiet house now to show for her mother's life and her mother's happiness and suffering, and nothing to show for Fay's harm," pp. 197-8), it has been emptied of memory. Ultimately, it is memory that redeems Laurel,

> She had been ready to hurt
> Fay. She had wanted to hurt her,
> had known herself capable of doing
> it. But such is the strangeness of
> the mind, it had been the memory of
> the child Wendell that had pre-
> vented her. (p. 206)

and allows her to put the past to rest.

> The past is no more open to help or
> hurt than was father in his cof-
> fin. The past is like him, imper-
> vious, and can never be awakened.
> It is memory that is the somnam-
> bulist. (p. 207)

Laurel can release the past, just as she can release her parents' house, because memory keeps it safe for her.

With an understanding of the past, Laurel comes to accept the inevitability of "blundering." Because her own marriage had been perfect in its brevity ("there had not happened a single blunder in their short life together," p. 189), Laurel is intolerant of the mob of people she hears at Mardi Gras ("the unmistakable sound of hundreds, of thousands, of people blundering," p. 55), her father's pallbearers ("she heard them blundering," p. 107), and Mr. Cheek ("Her mother had deplored his familiar ways and blundering hammer," p. 191). Laurel's acceptance of imperfection comes with her journey into the past. Her understanding does not condone the careless behavior she sees around her, but rather accepts it as the inescapable human error that comes of living. At the end of her night's vigil, therefore, Laurel weeps for the living perhaps more

147

than the dead: "She wept for what happened to life" (p. 181).

Laurel's resolution of the past is a product of listening to the silent voices of memory. In The Optimist's Daughter, the ability of language to order chaos is a process contained in memory. Laurel's acceptance of Fay in the final pages of the novel, for example, is stimulated by her memory of Wendell (p. 206), and the first night she spends in her room at Mount Salus is filled with the "velvety cloak of words" with which her parents unknowingly read her to sleep each night (p. 71). The books in her father's library similarly have their corresponding voices (p. 140), and the way in which Laurel knows that the funeral is being presided over is by the predominance of a single voice: "one voice dominated the rest: Miss Tennyson Bullock was taking charge" (p. 76). As Miss Tennyson's voice indicates, language orders chaos in the present as well as in memory. Judge McKelva relies on Laurel's voice to help structure time,

> She dropped her voice sometimes, and then sat still.
> 'I'm not asleep,' said her father. 'Please don't stop reading.' (p. 33)

just as Major Bullock relies on his own stories to order the chaos brought about by Judge McKelva's death and funeral (pp. 97-9). Laurel, however, does not understand the necessity of Major Bullock's tales about her father because she does not understand his intentions.

> 'Did you listen to their words?' she asked.
> 'They're being clumsy. Often because they were thinking of you.' (p. 100)

She is preoccupied instead with the literal truth or falsity of what he says and thus can neither comprehend nor sympathize with what she perceives as his lies about her father. Her response to Major Bullock is not unlike that to Dr. Bolt, whose words, like those of the Major, are intended to help order the chaos of Judge McKelva's death and funeral. Rather than helping Laurel, Dr. Bolt's words fail completely, and she does not hear them either time he speaks (pp. 107, 110). If

148

the language of Major Bullock and that of Dr. Bolt is incomprehensible to Laurel, then so is that of the community to Fay. When her family offers a ride home to Texas, therefore, Fay takes the opportunity to talk to those she understands best: " 'I'd just like to see somebody that can talk my language, that's my excuse' " (p. 117).

For Fay, Major Bullock, and ultimately Laurel herself, ordering chaos involves "telling it." Laurel realizes, at the beginning of her night's journey into the past, that she must "tell it" to be released.

> Even if you have kept silent for the sake of the dead, you cannot rest in your silence, as the dead rest. She listened to the wind, the rain, the blundering, frantic bird, and wanted to cry out as the nurse cried out to her, 'Abuse! Abuse!' (p. 155)

Yet, as we have said, her journey is one that is composed of the voices of memory and is primarily visual rather than verbal. The very difference of The Optimist's Daughter from Welty's other novels is its silence, the fact that Laurel finally does not "tell it" even though she knows that "to be released is to tell, unburden it" (p. 157). "Confiding the abuse to her mother," the only one Laurel could tell of Fay's guilt in her father's death, is finally impossible for Laurel because it would be an abuse far greater than Fay's. It is in arriving at pity for Fay that Laurel lays the ghosts of her parents to rest. For pity allows Laurel to complete the image of confluence she remembers earlier in the novel by placing Fay in the proper perspective. In other words, Laurel is able to move beyond judgment to acceptance of Fay through her understanding that Fay and Becky were each, in their own way, necessary to her father. Welty's statement, at the end of One Time, One Place, could therefore be that of Laurel herself.

> ... my wish, indeed my continuing passion, would be not to point the finger in judgment but to part a curtain, that invisible shadow that falls between people, the veil of indifference to each

> other's presence, each other's
> wonder,[22] each other's human
> plight.

In a sense, the end of Laurel's journey is to elude the
Labyrinth by seeing its pattern. It is with this knowledge that Laurel returns to Chicago at the end of the
novel, renewed and redeemed by her vision, and blessed
by Miss Adele's schoolchildren.

> The last thing Laurel saw, before
> they whirled into speed, was the
> twinkling of their hands, the many
> small and unknown hands, wishing
> her goodbye. (p. 208)

NOTES

[1]In his review, "The Continuity of Love" (<u>New Republic</u>, 10 June 1972, pp. 24-5), James Boatwright differentiates the Random House edition from that published in <u>The New Yorker</u> (1969): "To be specific, she has added 10,000 words, to the original 30,000, has changed names, altered the order of some scenes, subtly modified some of the characters, added much to our knowledge of the protagonist's past and present." This study will limit itself to the text first published as a novel by Random House.

[2]This preoccupation has been discussed most perceptively by John F. Desmond, in his "Pattern and Vision in <u>The Optimist's Daughter</u>." <u>A Still Moment: Essays on the Art of Eudora Welty</u>. Ed. John F. Desmond (London: The Scarecrow Press, Inc., 1978), pp. 118-138.

[3]Eudora Welty, <u>The Optimist's Daughter</u> (Greenwich, Conn.: Fawcett Publications, Inc., 1973), p. 9. Future references to this text will be included parenthetically after the quotation.

[4]Mircea Eliade, <u>Cosmos and History: The Myth of the Eternal Return</u> (New York: Harper and Row, 1954), p. 89.

[5]Guy Davenport, "Primal Visions." <u>National Review</u>, 22 June 1972, p. 697.

[6]Ibid.

[7]Mircea Eliade, <u>Cosmos and History: The Myth of the Eternal Return</u>, p. 17.

[8]Reynolds Price, "The Onlooker, Smiling: An Early Reading of <u>The Optimist's Daughter</u>." <u>Shenandoah</u>, 20 (Spring 1969), p. 73.

[9]John A. Allen, "Eudora Welty: The Three Moments." <u>A Still Moment</u>, p. 16.

[10]Reynolds Price, "The Onlooker, Smiling: An Early Reading of <u>The Optimist's Daughter</u>," p. 68.

[11]Guy Davenport, "Primal Visions," p. 697.

[12] Cleanth Brooks, "The Past Reexamined: The Optimist's Daughter." Mississippi Quarterly, xxvi (Fall 1973), p. 579.

[13] William F. Buckley, Jr. "The Southern Imagination: An Interview with Eudora Welty and Walker Percy." Mississippi Quarterly, xxvi (Fall 1973), p. 499.

[14] Laurel's "bridesmaids" serve a similar function. Important in the past (" 'The six of us right here, we were her bridesmaids,' " p. 66), these friends "show solidarity" (p. 63) not only by meeting Laurel at the train station (p. 61), reminiscing over her wedding (pp. 147-51), and driving Laurel to the airport (p. 207), but also by "grieving with" her (p. 151). It is in this sense that Welty refers to her collection of photographs (One Time, Once Place) as a "family album." The Eye of the Story (New York: Random House, 1978), p. 351.

[15] John A. Allen, "Eudora Welty: The Three Moments." A Still Moment, p. 26.

[16] Cleanth Brooks, in "The Past Reexamined: The Optimist's Daughter," sees Dalzells and Chisoms as balancing, rather than reinforcing, one another in the narrative: "The Dalzells are primitive, un-lettered, and earthy in their thought and speech, but they are not sleazily cheap; they are not on the make; they have not cut their connections with the land; they are family-minded. Mrs. Dalzell has nothing of the utter self-absorption of Fay" (p. 578).

[17] R. D. Laing, The Politics of the Family (Massey Lectures, 8th Series. Toronto: The Hunter Rose Company, Publishers, 1969), pp. 10-11. See the previous chapter, Losing Battles, p. 101, for Laing's definition of "mapping."

[18] Reynolds Price, "The Onlooker, Smiling: An Early Reading of The Optimist's Daughter," p. 60.

[19] This image (the turning pages as like ticks of a clock) recurs several pages later: "... he seemed to know when she turned each page, as though he kept up, through the succession of pages, with time, checking off moment after moment ..." (pp. 34-5).

[20]Eudora Welty, Preface to _One Time, One Place_. _The Eye of the Story_, p. 354.

[21] P. 15.

[22]Eudora Welty, Preface to _One Time, One Place_. _The Eye of the Story_, p. 355.

Obviously, the Southern Romance tradition extends beyond The Optimist's Daughter. Although centered in the experiences of the black Southerner, Toni Morrison's Song of Solomon (1977) and Alice Walker's Meridian (1976) belong to that tradition begun by the southern diarists over a century ago. "The living fairy tale" is thus as alive in each as it is in William Faulkner's Absalom, Absalom!: the confused legends and conflicting versions of the histories of his father and grandfather are as central to Milkman's life (and Morrison's novel) as are those of Thomas Sutpen to Quentin Compson (and Faulkner's novel). The preoccupations with family history and legend are linked in both works to the quest for identity that informs each novel as a whole.

Several elements in Morrison's Song of Solomon reinforce a predominant concern with name, and serve to place the work within the Southern Romance tradition. Circe's name and her function within the novel, for example, suggest an element of classical mythology, just as Macon Dead's name echoes the parallel element of regional mythology.[1] Milkman's quest for identity is closely aligned to a similar preoccupation with name, and both lead him to the grand and rotted farmhouse of his past. Finally, Pilate's gold earring (a talisman containing the written names of her family) and the sack of bones she suspends from her ceiling, are the objects that connect her to a family myth articulated through the prophecies and guidance of her dead father.

In Alice Walker's works, particularly Meridian, name and identity are closely aligned to what Welty sees as a "sense of place."[2] Meridian's name, from the definition that prefaces the novel to the end of the work, signifies an allegiance to the people and issues of the South, while the Copelands, in The Third Life of Grange Copeland (1970), gradually come to an understanding of the ambivalent nature of their feelings about "home." The generational movement of the Copelands toward an understanding of themselves within their region suggests a link between family and land that is ultimately another way of formulating Hunter Kay's maxim, "takes five generations to make a gentleman."[3] It is therefore not insignificant that Brownfield and Ruth are named as they are, and that the

155

novel ends with the patriarch's murder of his son and
his own sacrificial death.

Perhaps more than anything else, the Southern
Romance seeks to fuse time and place into significance.
In each of Welty's novels, and in subsequent Southern
novelists as well, the underlying need to create a
romance is the impulse behind the story as told, heard,
and repeated. It is Edna Earle's need to explain the
Ponders to the stranger who visits the Beulah Hotel,
just as it is the need of the Fairchilds in Delta Wedding and the Renfro-Beecham clan of Losing Battles to
repeat and re-work their particular legends through
family ritual. The elements of the Southern Romance --

1. reference to mythology born of, as John Crowe
    Ransom puts it, "classical and humanistic
    learning"
2. regional mythology surrounding the Southern
    character
3. geographic legend and folktale growing out
    of localities such as the Natchez Trace
4. inter- and intra-family graphing or hierar-
    chical structuring on the basis of myth as
    perpetuated by the Southern family
5. preoccupation with identity or name in rela-
    tion to the first families of the South
6. acceptance of narrator or story-teller as
    authority
7. repetition of, and preoccupation with,
    incident (whether the Civil War or a bit of
    family history)
8. belief in the ability of language to order
    chaos and the need to rewrite Southern
    history

incorporate the history of place with the history of a
people on both "actual" and "imaginary" levels (to borrow Hawthorne's distinctions). From the Southern
Civil War diarists through Eudora Welty's novels, the
need to create a Southern Romance is an attempt, among
other things, to justify a people to itself. The
Southern Romance therefore provides a way of coming to
terms, as Laurel Hand is forced to do in The Optimist's
Daughter, with ghosts both living and dead.

NOTES

[1] The reader will recall that Milkman's grandfather received his name through the carelessness of a drunken official: "He asked Papa where he was born. Papa said Macon. Then he asked him who his father was. Papa said, 'He's dead.' Asked him who owned him, Papa said, 'I'm free.' Well, the Yankee wrote it all down, but in the wrong spaces. Had him born in Dunfrie, wherever the hell that is, and in the space for his name the fool wrote 'Dead' comma 'Macon.' " Song of Solomon (New York: New American Library, 1977), p. 53.

[2] See Eudora Welty, "Place in Fiction" (The Eye of the Story. New York: Random House, 1978), pp. 116-133.

[3] Hunter Kay, "The Fifth Generation." Stories of the Modern South, p. 183.

[4] The Custom House introduction to The Scarlet Letter (New York: New American Library, 1959), p. 45.

BIBLIOGRAPHY

Adams, James L. Conceptual Blockbusting. San Francisco: San Francisco Book Co., 1976.

Aldridge, John W. "Eudora Welty: Metamorphosis of a Southern Lady Writer." Saturday Review, 11 April 1970, pp. 21-23, 35-36.

Appel, Alfred, Jr. A Season of Dreams: The Fiction of Eudora Welty. Baton Rouge: Louisiana State University Press, 1965.

A Belle of the Fifties: Memoirs of Mrs. Clay of Alabama, Covering Social and Political Life in Washington and the South, 1853-1866, Put into Narrative Form by Ada Sterling. New York: Doubleday, 1905.

Bishop, John Peale. "The Violent Country: The Robber Bridegroom," The Collected Essays of John Peale Bishop. Ed. Edmund Wilson. New York: Scribner's 1948.

Black, Max. Models and Metaphors. Ithaca and London: Cornell University Press, 1962.

Blackwell, Louise. "Eudora Welty and the Rubber Fence Family." Kansas Magazine, 30 (1965).

Boatwright, James. "The Continuity of Love." New Republic, 166 (10 June 1972), pp. 24-25.

_____. "I Call This a Reunion to Remember, All!" New York Times Book Review, 12 April 1970, pp. 1, 32-34.

Brooks, Cleanth. "The Past Reexamined: The Optimist's Daughter." Mississippi Quarterly, xxvi (Fall 1973), pp. 577-587.

Brown, Ashley. "Eudora Welty and the Mythos of Summer." Shenandoah, 20 (Spring 1969).

Brunvand, Jan Harold. The Study of American Folklore: An Introduction, 2nd Ed. New York: W. W. Norton and Company, Inc., 1968.

Bryant, J. A., Jr. *Eudora Welty*. University of
    Minnesota Pamphlets on American Writers (No.
    66); Univ. of Minn. Press, Minneapolis, 1968.

Cassirer, Ernst. *The Philosophy of Symbolic Forms*, 3
    vols., Vol 2, *Mythical Thought*. New Haven:
    Yale University Press, 1955.

Chase, Richard. *The American Novel and Its Tradition*.
    London: G. Bell and Sons, 1957).

Chesnut, Mary Boykin. *A Diary from Dixie*. Ed.
    Isabella D. Martin, Myrta Lockett Avary. New
    York: D. Appleton & Co., 1905.

The Civil War in Song and Story, 1860-1865, collected
    and arranged by Frank Moore. New York: Johnson
    Reprint Corporation, 1970.

Clark, Charles C. "*The Robber Bridegroom*: Realism and
    Fantasy on the Natchez Trace." *Mississippi*
    Quarterly, xxvi (1973), 625-638.

"Cloud-Cuckoo Symphony." *Time*, 47 (22 April 1946), pp.
    104, 106, 108.

Coates, Robert M. *The Outlaw Years: The History of the*
    Land Pirates of the Natchez Trace. New York:
    Macauley, 1930.

The Complete Grimm's Fairy Tales. Ed. Joseph Campbell,
    trans. Margaret Hunt. New York: Pantheon
    Books, 1944.

Davenport, F. Garvin, Jr. *The Myth of Southern*
    History: Historical Consciousness in
    Twentieth-Century Literature. Nashville:
    Vanderbilt University Press, 1967.

Davenport, Guy. "Primal Visions." *National Review*, 23
    June 1972, p. 697.

Davis, Charles E. "The South in Eudora Welty's
    Fiction: A Changing World." *Studies in*
    American Fiction, 3 (Autumn 1975), pp. 199-209.

Dawson, Sarah Morgan. *A Confederate Girl's Diary*.
    Bloomington: Indiania University Press, 1960.

Desmond, John F. Ed. A Still Moment: Essays on the
    Art of Eudora Welty. London: The Scarecrow
    Press, Inc., 1978.

Drake, Robert Y., Jr. "The Reasons of the Heart."
    Georgia Review, 11 (Winter 1957).

Dusenbury, Winifred. "Baby Doll and The Ponder Heart."
    Modern Drama, 3 (February 1961).

Eliade, Mircea. Cosmos and History: The Myth of the
    Eternal Return. New York: Harper and Row,
    1954.

Faulkner, William. Absalom! Absalom! New York:
    Modern Library, 1936.

_____. The Unvanquished. New York:
    Vintage Books, 1934.

French, Warren. "A Note on Eudora Welty's The Ponder
    Heart." College English, 15 (May 1954).

Frye, Northrop. The Secular Scripture: A Study of the
    Structure of Romance. Cambridge: Harvard
    University Press, 1976.

Gossett, Louise Y. "Eudora Welty's New Novel: The
    Comedy of Loss." Southern Literary Journal, 3
    (Fall 1970), pp. 122-137.

Hamilton, Edith. Mythology. New York: New American
    Library, 1940.

Hardy, John Edward. "Delta Wedding as Region and
    Symbol." Sewanee Review, 60 (July-Sept. 1952),
    pp. 397-417.

Harrison, Mrs. Burton. Recollections Grave and Gay.
    New York: Scribner's, 1911.

Hawthorne, Nathaniel. The Custom House introduction to
    The Scarlet Letter. New York: New American
    Library, 1959.

Heisenberg, Werner. Physics and Philosophy: The
    Revolution in Modern Science. New York: Harper
    & Row, 1958.

Heroines of Dixie: Spring of High Hopes. Ed.
Katherine M. Jones. New York: Ballantine
Books, 1955.

Hoffman, Daniel G. Form and Fable in American Fiction.
New York: Oxford University Press, 1961.

Holland, Robert B. "Dialogue as a Reflection of Place
in The Ponder Heart." American Literature, 35
(Nov. 1963).

Howell, Elmo. "Eudora Welty's Comedy of Manners."
South Atlantic Quarterly, 69 (Autumn 1970), pp.
469-477.

Humanities Report. May 1979, Vol. 1, No. 5. "The
Sciences and the Humanities: Kindred
Activities."

I'll Take My Stand: The South and the Agrarian
Tradition, by Twelve Southerners. New York:
Harper and Brothers, 1930.

Invisible Loyalties: Reciprocity in Intergenerational
Family Therapy. Eds. Ivan Boszormenyi-Nagy and
Geraldine Spark. New York: Medical Dept.,
Harper & Row, 1975.

Isaacs, Neil D. Eudora Welty. Austin, Texas: Steck-
Vaughn Co.: Southern Writers Series, #8, 1969.

Jaynes, Julian. The Origin of Consciousness in the
Breakdown of the Bicameral Mind. Boston:
Houghton Mifflin Co., 1977.

Jones, Howard Mumford. "On Leaving the South."
Scribner's LXXXIX (Jan. 1931).

Karanikas, Alexander. Tillers of a Myth: Southern
Agrarians as Social and Literary Critics.
Madison: University of Wisconsin Press, 1966).

Kemble, Frances Anne. Journal of a Residence on a
Georgia Plantation in 1838-1839. Chicago:
Afro-Am Press, 1969.

Kroll, Jack. "The Lesson of the Master." Newsweek, 13
April 1970, pp. 90-91.

Laing, R. D. _The Politics of the Family._ Massey
    Lectures, Eighth Series. Canadian Broadcasting
    Corp., CBC Learning Systems, Box 500, Toronto,
    Canada 116. The Hunter Rose Co., Publishers,
    1969.

Laing, R. D. A. Esterson, _Sanity, Madness, and the_
    Family. London: Tavistock Publications, Std.,
    2nd ed. 1970; 1st ed. 1964.

Landess, Thomas H. "More Trouble in Mississippi:
    Family Vs. Antifamily in Miss Welty's _Losing_
    Battles." _Sewanee Review_, 79 (Oct.-Dec. 1971),
    pp. 626-634.

Lewis, R.W.B. _The American Adam: Innocence, Tragedy,_
    and Tradition in the Nineteenth Century.
    Chicago: University of Chicago Press, 1955.

Lively, Robert A. _Fiction Fights the Civil War: An_
    Unfi nished Chapter in the Literary History of
    the American People. Chapel Hill: The
    University of North Carolina Press, 1957.

Lubbock, Percy. _The Craft of Fiction._ New York:
    Viking Press, 1957.

Mitchell, Lt. Col. Joseph B. _Military Leaders in the_
    Civil War. New York: G. P. Putnam's Sons,
    1972.

Mississippi Quarterly: The Journal of Southern
    Culture. Vol. XXVI, No. 4, Fall 1973. Special
    Issue: Eudora Welty.

Moss, Howard. "Eudora Welty's New Novel About Death
    and Class." _New York Times Book Review_, 21 May
    1972, pp. 1, 18.

Murray, Henry A. _Myth and Mythmaking._ New York:
    George Braziller, Inc., 1960.

Myers, Robert Manson. _The Children of Pride: A True_
    Story of Virginia and the Civil War. New Haven:
    Yale University Press, 1972.

Myths, Rites, Symbols: A Mircea Eliade Reader. Eds.
    Wendell C. Beane and William G. Doty, Vol. 1.
    New York: Harper & Row, 1976.

Oates, Joyce Carol. "Eudora's Web." Atlantic, 225 (April 1970), pp. 118-120, 122.

Osterweis, Rollin G. The Myth of the Lost Cause 1865-1900. Archon Books, New York: The Shoe String Press, Inc., 1973.

_____. Romanticism and Nationalism in the Old South. New Haven: Yale University Press, 1949.

Pearson, Edmund. Dime Novels; Or, Following an Old Trail in Popular Literature. Port Washington, New York: Kennikat Press, Inc., 1929.

Perry, John Weir, M.D. The Far Side of Madness. Englewood Cliffs: Prentice-Hall, Inc., 1974.

Prenshaw, Peggy. "Cultural Patterns in Eudora Welty's Delta Wedding and 'The Demonstrators.' " Notes on Mississippi Writers, 3 (Fall 1970), pp. 51-68.

Price, Reynolds. "The Onlooker, Smiling: An Early Reading of The Optimist's Daughter." Shenandoah, 20 (Spring 1969), pp. 58-73.

The Psychological Interior of the Family. Ed. Gerald Handel. Chicago: Aldine Publishing Co., 1967.

Ransom, John Crowe. "Delta Fiction." Kenyon Review, 8 (Summer 1946), pp. 503-507.

Rosenfeld, Isaac. "Double Standard." New Republic, 114 (20 April 1946), pp. 633-634.

Rubin, Louis D. Jr. "Everything Brought Out in the Open: Eudora Welty's Losing Battles." Hollins Critic, 7 (June 1970), pp. 1-12.

Sapir, Edward. Language: An Introduction to the Study of Speech. New York: Harcourt, Brace, Jovanovich, 1921.

Scholes, Robert. Kellogg, Robert. The Nature of Narrative. London: Oxford University Press, 1966.

Scott, Anne Firor. The Southern Lady: From Pedestal